920
MOR

93-7008

MOREY, JANET

Famous Asian Americans

ECIA Chapter II

Famous
Asian
Americans

Famous

Asian
Americans

Janet Nomura Morey

& Wendy Dunn

ILLUSTRATED WITH PHOTOGRAPHS

Cobblehill Books

DUTTON   NEW YORK

FCIA CH 2

Photographs are used by permission of All-Sport Photography, 18; Courtesy of Jose Aruego, 3, 5, 8, 12; Michael Baz, 21; CBS: Tony Esparza, 29, Patrick Pagnano, 30; Chicago Mercantile Exchange, 46; Private collection, Myung-Whun Chung, 36, 39; © 1984 Goldcrest Films and Television Limited, All Rights Reserved, 93; Courtesy of Dr. Wendy Gramm, 56; Photograph by Evelyn Hofer, 130; K. Horiuchi, 136 (bottom); Courtesy ICM Artists, Ltd., 34; Courtesy of Daniel K. Inouye, 60, 63, 65, 67; Courtesy of June Kuramoto, 87; © Peter Menzel, 144, 148; NASA, Onizuka family photo, 118, 123, 125; Courtesy of Dustin Nguyen, 107, 110; Alan Porter, 51; Photo by Vivianne Purdom, 41; Courtesy of Sundary Rama, 98, 101; Steve Sakai, 84; © Franco Salmoiraghi, 71; Ezra Stoller © Esto, 136 (top); Kaz Takeuchi, 81; Jay Thompson, 89; Marsha Traeger, © 1989 *Los Angeles Times*, 76; Courtesy of Wang Laboratories, Inc. 1990, 152, 156, 158. Map by Susan Detrich.

Library of Congress Cataloging-in-Publication Data
Morey, Janet.
Famous Asian Americans / Janet Nomura Morey and Wendy Dunn.
p. cm.
Includes bibliographical references and index.
Summary: Chronicles the lives and accomplishments of fourteen
Asian Americans including Jose Aruego, Michael Chang, An
Wang, and Ellison Onizuka.
ISBN 0-525-65080-6
1. Asian Americans—Biography—Juvenile literature. [1. Asian
Americans—Biography.] I. Dunn, Wendy. II. Title.
E184.06M67 1992
920′.009295073—dc20 91-17255 CIP AC

Published in the United States by Cobblehill Books,
an affiliate of Dutton Children's Books,
a division of Penguin Books USA Inc.
375 Hudson Street, New York, New York 10014

Designed by Mina Greenstein
Printed in the United States of America
First Edition   10 9 8 7 6 5 4 3 2

Acknowledgments

We would like to thank our editor for continued encouragement and assistance throughout this project. We are also grateful to Dr. Harry H. L. Kitano for contributing the Foreword and providing insight into the backgrounds of the prominent people in this book.

We greatly appreciate the interviews and assistance granted by the following participants in this book: Jose Aruego, Wendy Lee Gramm, June Kuramoto, Haing Ngor, Dustin Nguyen, and Samuel Ting.

We also thank the following: Michael Chang and his parents, Joe and Betty Chang; Lorene Sabatino, Administrative Assistant to Jerry Solomon of ProServ; Connie Chung; Catherine Upin, CBS News Press Representative; Myung-Whun Chung, his staff assistants at the Opera de la Bastille, and ICM Artists, Ltd.; Allison Adams, assistant to Dr. Gramm; Daniel K. Inouye; Michele Konishi of Senator Inouye's office and Gregg Takayama, press assistant; Tim Schaffner, literary agent for Maxine Hong Kingston; Gail Matsui of the Japanese American Cultural and Community Center, for helping with June Kuramoto's chapter; Sundary Rama, who loaned photographs of Dr. Ngor, and The Marion Rosenberg Office; Jay D. Schwartz and Felice Sands of Baker, Winokur, Ryder Public Relations, for their assistance with Dustin Nguyen's chapter; Lorna Onizuka, widow of Ellison S. Onizuka, and Matt Matsuoka, who assisted with Ellison S. Onizuka's chapter; I. M. Pei; Office of Communications, Pei Cobb Freed & Partners; Paul Guzzi, Senior Vice President, his secretary Donna Marion, and Gail Jackson, Public Relations Consultant, all of Wang Laboratories; Janet Minami, Director, Media Services, and Warren Furutani, School Board Member, both of the Los Angeles Unified School District; Jeanne Akashi, Director, Asian Pacific American Education Commission, Los Angeles; and Marjorie Lee and library staff, UCLA Asian American Studies Center Reading Room.

We especially appreciate the support of members of our families, Jack Morey, Bruce Dunn, and Julie Dunn. We also extend special thanks to Allen Michel, our legal advisor; and Kitty Ando and Jessica Roll, for technical assistance.

Preface

People from Asian countries have been coming to American shores for generations and for many reasons. Some have sought better economic opportunity, such as the Chinese laborers attracted by the California Gold Rush and many Japanese who came several decades later. Some others fled war in their homelands, such as recent refugees from Vietnam and Cambodia. Many Asian Americans were born here in the United States, and others immigrated. Many Asians continue to come. Asian-American contributions will continue to grow.

This book chronicles the lives of fourteen outstanding Asian Americans. The story of each family or individual move from an Asian country is told, childhood remembrances and motivations are conveyed, and the significance of each achievement is fully explained. In many of the chapters, these experiences are related in the person's own words, from interviews conducted by the authors. In other cases, family members or assistants offered insights and information. Photographs, often from personal collections, highlight each entry. All the subjects, or their designated aides, have approved the material in their own chapter.

The number of distinguished Asian Americans is great. These fourteen represent a variety of professions and backgrounds. They have achieved prominence in government, architecture, science, the arts, business, media, and sports. They include:

—a Nobel-Prize-winning physicist who has discovered secrets of the atom
—a teen-age tennis star who won the French Open
—a doctor who escaped from Cambodia and became an Oscar-winning actor in Hollywood
—an architect whose achievements are recognized internationally
—an astronaut who died tragically with the explosion of the space shuttle *Challenger*

The fourteen individuals or their families came from China, Japan, Korea, Vietnam, Cambodia, or the Philippines, some of the countries which have provided a great proportion of immigrants from eastern Asia to the United States.

Pacific Rim countries are increasingly at the forefront of current events, and young readers will hear more about them in the coming years. The individuals presented in this book are of these heritages and offer among the finest examples of striving, excellence, and contribution. This volume serves to inspire a new, young audience. As they meet these significant Asian Americans, they will understand more about the heritage and influence of each.

Contents

Foreword

At the present time, Asian Americans are a more visible force than they were in the past. It was not that long ago that they were considered an invisible minority, small in number and concentrated along the West Coast and in Hawaii, and far removed from the American mainstream. They were considered quaint and not able to fit into American society. These perceptions were reinforced by lack of personal contact, and negative portrayals in the movies and the mass media.

Many of these images remain. Although the term Asian American covers well over twenty different groups, each with their own history, language, and culture, there is the tendency to think that they are a homogeneous group. As a consequence, Chinese are mistaken for Koreans, who are in turn mistaken to be Japanese. The view that they are interchangeable reinforces the stereotype that because they all look alike, they must be alike.

Another misperception is that Asian Americans, even those born and raised in the United States, still have an intimate tie with the land of their ancestors. There is the belief that an Asian face guarantees a thorough knowledge of an Asian language and culture, so that even members of the fourth or fifth generation hear the comment, "But where did you learn how to speak English?" One tragic consequence of this image was the wartime evacuation of the Japanese, the majority of whom were American-born citizens, but who nevertheless were placed in concentration camps because of their presumed tie with Japan.

The Chinese were the first Asian immigrant group; they arrived during the California Gold Rush in the 1840s and '50s. A fear of economic competition from Chinese workers developed, and there was also racism against the Chinese. They soon faced discrimination. As Asians, they were not permitted to become naturalized American citizens; only those actually born in the United States could become citizens. Local laws levied taxes on their work, and they were forced to pay fines for living in buildings which were too crowded. Chinese were also targeted for acts of violence. Growing anti-Chinese sentiment finally resulted in the Chinese Exclusion Act of 1882, which banned Chinese immigration. The ban was lifted in 1943—the Chinese were our allies in World War II—a token quota was granted, and they were permitted to become naturalized citizens. The 1965 Immigration Act, which abolished national-origins quotas, provided the impetus for significant Chinese immigration to the United States. In 1960, prior to the new Act, there were over 200,000 Chinese in the United States; in 1985, there was an estimated one million in the country.

The reality of discrimination had several effects. The Chinese were forced into segregated living—the "Chinatowns"—and the ban on immigration meant an unbalanced sex ratio with a high proportion of males. For the most part, family life, including an American-born generation of children, was delayed for many decades. But, it should be noted that today there are some fourth- and fifth-generation descendants of the early pioneers, as well as large numbers of recent ethnic Chinese immigrants from a variety of areas, such as Hong Kong, mainland China, Taiwan, the Philippines, and Southeast Asia. So what may appear to be a homogeneous group is in reality a population characterized by diversity.

The Japanese followed the Chinese into the United States. In the later part of the 1800s, many Japanese in rural areas faced hardship caused by changes in the Japanese economy as that country modernized. By 1885, the government of Japan changed its policy which had not allowed Japanese to emigrate. Once they were permitted to leave, many who sought better economic opportunity went to the United States. They began arriving in the 1890s, and by 1920 there were over 110,000 Japanese, primarily in California. There was also significant immigration to Hawaii, annexed by the United States in 1898 and later granted statehood in 1959.

The Japanese faced discrimination soon after their arrival. They and other Asian immigrants could not become citizens, and many state and local laws were passed which prohibited "aliens ineligible for citizenship" from owning land (Alien Land Laws). Also, Japanese and other Asians were subjected to various segregation laws. Under the Gentlemen's Agreement of 1907-08 between Japan and the United States, Japanese immigration was restricted. By 1924, they, as well as residents of other Asian countries, were excluded from immigration. However, unlike the Chinese, many were able to start family life in the United States, since they sent for women from Japan (the "picture brides") and started an American-born generation (the Nisei). Under this Gentlemen's Agreement, Japan restricted the immigration of its laborers to the United States, but it permitted those already in America to send for family members, including wives. Sometimes, these were arranged marriages where photographs were first exchanged, explaining why the women were called "picture brides."

The World War II evacuation of the Japanese (1942-45) marked a high point of discrimination. More than 110,000 persons of Japanese ancestry, the majority of them American-born citizens, were herded into ten camps in isolated, deserted areas in Arkansas, Arizona, Wyoming, Colorado, Utah, and California. It is to the credit of many of these people, with the aid of both houses of Congress and the executive branch of the government, that a redress bill was passed. Those who were incarcerated during World War II and were alive at the signing of the bill were to receive $20,000 each from entitlement funds, starting in 1990.

The Japanese were the most numerous Asian-American group in the 1970 census. However, by 1980, they were already behind the Filipino (some prefer to use the term "Pilipino") and the Chinese. This trend has occurred primarily because of declining birth rates and the lack of immigration from the old country.

The Filipinos followed the Chinese and Japanese to the United States. The Filipinos had lived under colonial rule, first by the Spanish and then by the Americans. During Spanish rule, many Filipinos received Spanish surnames, especially after an 1849 decree by Narciso Claveria, governor of the Philippines at that time. Claveria wanted those who did not already have a family name to adopt one from a long list sent out. As governor, Claveria was appointed by and responsible to the King of Spain, and he returned to Spain after his term in the Philippines. The Filipinos were later ruled by the Americans, as a result of the Spanish-American War of 1898. The early history of the American experience in the Philippines was characterized by guerrilla warfare, atrocities, and constant conflict. However, because of their colonized status, Filipinos were exempt from Asian Exclusion legislation, so that by 1930, there were over 30,000 in the United States and an additional 63,000 in the Territory of Hawaii. As with other Asians, they faced discrimination. The immigration loophole was closed by the Tydings-McDuffie Act of 1934 which promised independence for the Philippines in 1945, but which placed an annual quota of fifty Filipino immigrants.

In 1985, an estimated one million Filipinos made them one of the most numerous Asian groups in the

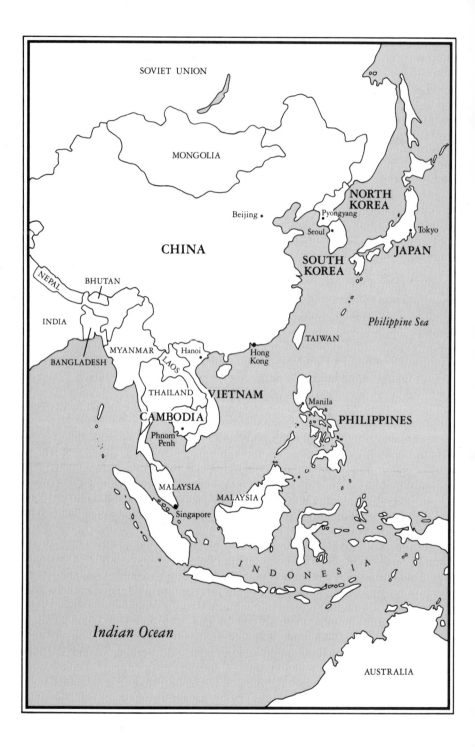

United States. The old immigration was characterized by single, male laborers; the current migration includes a large number of professionals, especially in the health fields.

The passage of the 1965 Immigration Act has also meant a large migration of Koreans. Whereas in 1970, there was an estimated 70,000 residents, the 1980 census recorded over 350,000 and an estimated 542,000 in 1985. Although they have built a large-scale Koreatown in Los Angeles, they have also settled throughout the United States. Many have entered the small business field; much of their migration has been family centered, so that the talents of the entire family have often been utilized. Instances of conflict with other disadvantaged minorities has been a problem.

The other large-scale migration of Asians has been from Southeast Asia, which includes Vietnam, Cambodia, and Laos. The war in Vietnam created a vast number of refugees; from 1974 to 1984, more than 700,000 Southeast Asians were admitted to the United States. Refugees have also been admitted to France, Canada, Australia, China, West Germany, and Great Britain.

Numerous Southeast Asians have entered the United States at a time when many of the institutional barriers, such as restrictive laws and rigid social patterns, have receded. However, they have also faced tightening budgets in the United States and increased competition for jobs. They have been characterized by ethnic diversity. It appears much too early to assess their adaptation to the new society.

In summary, Asians arrived in different numbers, for different reasons, with different cultures and with different historical experiences. They faced common barriers—they could not become citizens, could not own land, were restricted in housing, jobs, and the use of public facilities. They also faced laws against marriage between races, so that prejudice, discrimination, and segregation were consistent experiences. Nevertheless, Asians were able to achieve a degree of upward mobility, and many have achieved a relatively comfortable status as opportunities in the larger society became more open, and as institutional barriers were overcome. Chinese immigrants could not become naturalized citizens until 1943, and Filipinos not until 1946. In 1952, racial and ethnic barriers to immigration and naturalization were removed by the McCarran-Walter Act. Japanese, Koreans, Vietnamese, Cambodians, and other immigrants who had not been able to become naturalized American citizens now were eligible. Once they were eligible to become citizens, they could also own land. Other laws based on race were later changed. These included restrictive state marriage laws, which were voided by the United States Supreme Court in 1967. It is important that Asian Americans remain active and alert to instances of prejudice and discrimination, so that the gains of the past are not allowed to slip away.

The individuals that you will read about in this volume represent a variety of experiences, and the types of barriers that they as Asian Americans have had to face. These Americans of Asian ancestry have contributed greatly to

America. Their courage and humanity should serve as an inspiration for future generations of Americans.

HARRY H. L. KITANO, Ph.D.
Los Angeles, California

Dr. Harry H. L. Kitano was born in San Francisco, California. He received his Ph.D. from the University of California, Berkeley. He is Professor of Social Welfare and Sociology at the University of California, Los Angeles (UCLA), and also holds the Endowed Chair of Japanese American Studies. He has also been a visiting professor at the International Christian University in Tokyo, the University of Bristol in England, and the University of Hawaii. He is the author of numerous articles, and his books include *Asian Americans: Emerging Minorities* (with Roger Daniels); *Race Relations; Japanese Americans: The Evolution of a Subculture*; and *American Racism* (with Roger Daniels).

Jose Aruego

Jose Espiritu Aruego was destined to become an attorney. His father, Jose Maminta Aruego, was a prominent attorney in the Philippines, where the family lived. The elder Mr. Aruego wrote legal books and participated in important constitutional conventions. Young Jose was born in Manila, the capital of the Philippines, on August 9, 1932. As he grew up, it was understood that he, too, would become a lawyer. His sister, Gloria, and many of his friends became lawyers. Jose earned his law degree as expected, passed the bar exam, and went to work.

Yet there was another side to young Jose Aruego that was soon to change his life. He had always loved to doodle. In school, he had enjoyed decorating the bulletin boards, chalkboards, and classrooms. "All kids, when young, like to draw, and if they are known for it, feel good," Jose Aruego has said. He remembers thinking, "If I am good at drawing, people notice me." He collected comic books and was very interested in their artwork.

Jose became a lawyer, following his family's tradition, but he was not enthusiastic about the profession. He really wanted to be an artist, especially one who drew comic books and cartoons. Very quickly, he quit law and began his training all over again, but this time in graphic arts. Today, Jose Aruego still marvels that his childhood dreams are now his adult life. As a writer and illustrator of children's picture books, he combines his love of humor and animals with his talent for drawing. He is delighted that children enjoy his stories and pictures as much as he enjoys creating them.

Over sixty books have been illustrated by Jose Aruego. He wrote at least ten of those, while the remainder were by other authors. His pictures have strong lines and bright colors. They can tell a story all by themselves, with very few words, or richly portray memorable characters and humorous situations. He drew huge crocodile teeth, picked clean by a little bird, in his *Symbiosis: A Book of Unusual Friendships*. That imaginatively helped show what symbiosis is, a relationship between two different types of living beings, especially when both of them benefit. He wrote and drew the frenzied competition between two carabaos (water buffalo) in *Look What I Can Do*. For author Robert Kraus, he showed the frustration in the face of the little tiger Leo in *Leo the Late Bloomer*, and the confusion of Owliver, the owl trying to decide on a career for himself in *Owliver*.

*Jose Aruego at
about age six*

"I do a lot of animals," Mr. Aruego explains. "One of the reasons is that I often visited and spent summers at a farm in Dangasina, about three hours from Manila." The family animals included about six cats, their kittens, as many dogs, their puppies, some horses, chickens, ducks, frogs, tadpoles, and three pigs. Jose wanted a pet of his own, but he was not lucky and each time he tried to take care of a pet, the animal would die. His parents remedied this situation by having relatives actually keep and care for pets which they said belonged to Jose. In this way, Jose was satisfied, and the pets stayed healthy and survived. When Jose would doodle for pleasure, he drew playful animals, not just random squiggles.

As Jose was growing up, his father was a professor of law at the University of Manila. At a young age, Jose learned about politics. He began to prepare for a life similar to his father's, even though young Jose's own legal career turned out to be very, very short. One of his boyhood friends, however, did become deeply involved in politics. That friend was Benigno Aquino. The two boys sat near each other in class because the students were placed in alphabetical order. Benigno Aquino later became a political leader opposed to President Ferdinand Marcos of the Philippines. Mr. Aquino was assassinated in 1983, gunned down at the airport in Manila. His widow, Corazon Aquino, became president of the Philippines several years later, in 1986.

Jose Aruego's family was immersed in the law and government, but Jose also enjoyed comic books, collected them, and even rented them to his friends. He liked their bold artwork and has said that he still envisions some of his own art telling a story in panels, just as comic books do. The comic books were eventually what brought Jose to New York. He attended the University of the Philippines, receiving his Bachelor of Arts degree in 1953, and then the anticipated law degree in 1955, but already he was discontent. He did not study particularly hard for the bar exam, which a person must pass in order to practice law. He did not do very well, but he did pass. However, he was not so lucky in his first case, and it turned out to be his last. He lost, and after only three months in law, he decided to totally switch careers. Jose's father realized that his son wanted art and was very supportive of his wishes. He even suggested that Jose go to Paris, where many artists study. But Jose really wanted

Dressed in cap and gown, Jose Aruego walks down steps after receiving his law degree.

the type of art created for comic books, and this was best learned in New York.

Jose Aruego enrolled at the Parsons School of Design in New York City. Initially, the distant move was hard for him. He remembers, "At first, I wanted to go home right away; I had to adapt. I missed friends, family." He adjusted, though, and traveled even farther. He studied art in Europe for a summer and became fascinated with line drawings, a technique he now uses in his own illustrations. In 1959, he graduated from Parsons with a certificate in graphic arts and advertising. He soon went to work in a studio, decorating Christmas angel mannequins by gluing feathers on their wings. He worked for several design studios, advertising agencies, and magazines for about six years. He traveled in the United States and in many other countries as part of a group interested in international friendship. Back in New York City, he painted an enormous mural of that city at International House on Riverside Drive. He also met another artist, Ariane Dewey, and they married in 1961.

During much of this time, Jose was also drawing cartoons and submitting them to magazines. They began to sell to *Saturday Evening Post*, *Look*, and *The New Yorker*. Each new sale fetched a higher price, so Jose left his job and became a full-time cartoonist. He worked free-lance, so he was not employed by any one magazine. He offered his work to several publications and was paid for each cartoon used. He enjoyed the drawing, but became discouraged at the rate of rejection. He has estimated that only one in twenty of an artist's cartoons may be accepted, making it difficult to keep a sense of humor.

While cartooning for magazines, Jose also wrote and illustrated a children's book. This was about the time his son, Juan, was born. It is not easy to have a book accepted, either, and Jose's first book was rejected by the first publisher to whom it was shown. An editor at another publishing house especially liked his illustrations, however, and that book, *The King and His Friends*, was published in 1969 and dedicated to Juan. In the book, the king was named "Doowah," which was actually the name of little Juan's security blanket. Another book written by Jose used his son's name in the title, *Juan and the Asuangs*.

Jose Aruego was immediately successful in the field of children's books. His second book, in 1970, was illustrated for writer Robert Kraus. That book, *Whose Mouse Are You?*, was honored as an American Library Association Notable Book selection. Jose had a total of five books published in 1970. Three were illustrations for other authors, but two were entirely his own. One of his own was *Juan and the Asuangs*, which won an award as an outstanding picture book of the year from *The New York Times*. These were among the first of many awards in his career. During these early years, Jose also collaborated with his wife, Ariane Aruego. Together, they wrote and illustrated *A Crocodile's Tale*, and they illustrated several books for other writers. Although the Aruegos were divorced in 1973, they have continued to collaborate, but Ariane has resumed her maiden name, Ariane Dewey.

For over twenty years, Jose Aruego has charmed both children and adults with his stories and antic animals. He explains, "I have written mostly animal stories. The

The artist in his apartment studio, 1971

ideas must have humor. They must take off from something funny. If they are serious, I cannot get my juices working. Kids like to be happy and my books give them the opportunity."

When he is the illustrator for another writer's story, Mr. Aruego still relies on humor, but his role is different. "A writer submits a manuscript to the editor. The editor looks for an illustrator, or the writer can recommend someone. I work with an editor and seldom see the writer. The editor knows exactly what the writer wants, but gives me a free hand. The writer sees the whole piece. If the writer wants to make a major comment, he or she works with the editor."

Mr. Aruego has described how a picture book is created, whether from one of his own stories or someone else's. "First, I have an idea and make a drawing, a fast drawing. A picture book is usually thirty-two pages, so I have to tell a story in thirty-two pages. Book pages are in multiples of eight. I show a dummy to the editor. The editor knows how I work, and can envision the finished work. When I started, I had to make finished drawings. Now I do sixteen drawings and two of the spreads are final. With the drawings, I talk to the editor and see what she wants. I finish in watercolor. Before modern technology, artists had to separate colors. For my first books I had to separate colors. Now they can shoot full-color work."

Mr. Aruego lives and works in an apartment in New York City. His home is filled with antiques, plants, and art supplies. The frame of an old four-poster bed is used as a display for plants, and an antique pinball machine is part of his collection. Jose Aruego is usually involved with several books at the same time. He often begins his day at 4:00 A.M. and explains, "I work in the morning, very early. In the afternoon, I do research. The earlier I get up, the more I get done. I have a studio in my apartment." Small, detailed sketches drawn by Mr. Aruego are tacked to the wall near his drawing board. He creates his actual book illustrations much larger, but based on these original ideas.

With its lush foliage and many ornamental pieces from the Philippines, Jose Aruego's apartment reflects his heritage. He feels that his drawings and stories also stem from his Philippine culture, adding, "Someone told me my drawings are very tropical. The lines are like calligraphy at home in the Philippines, and the background art is very decorative." Some of his tales are written from Philippine folklore. They sometimes include terms from native language, such as the names of the spirits in *Juan and the Asuangs*. Mr. Aruego speaks both Tagalog and English.

Jose Aruego still visits the Philippines, but feels very much an American. Wanting to become an American citizen, he said, "Here I want to vote. I like it here with politics. I have been here quite some time. My culture is here now." He recalls when he first moved to New York, and how he missed everyone back home, but then adds, "Now I have different ideas. I still have old friends, but we have very little in common."

Jose Aruego changed both his country and his career.

Looking back, he admits, "Going to law school was a waste, but it helped—I have discipline. In law you do a lot of research, and that kind of thing helped. My work is like doing a thesis with pictures, only it is more fun. My agent handles contracts," he laughingly adds. "When I went into law, it was the old school, to want a profession that is safe." Now he says it is more common for children to want jobs that are more unusual. If parents and children differ, he thinks they should "compromise."

In 1976, Jose Aruego was selected Outstanding Filipino Abroad in Arts, and he considered the honor very special, explaining, "When I got the award from Marcos and went home, it was nice being recognized in my new profession. Lots of my lawyer classmates and professors were proud that I made it as an illustrator. I changed professions and changed to what is successful."

He eagerly offers advice to children who think they would like to be artists. "Art has so many facets—books, magazines—one should go where their talent lies. Some are good artists but cannot tell stories. If you intend drawing as your profession, you must be ready to compromise. There is that word again. You cannot always do what you want. In the beginning, you have to adjust your style to earn money. Do what you want on the side. The most beautiful thing is doing what you want when that earns money."

Jose Aruego admires other artists and illustrators such as Tomi Ungerer. He notes that Donald Crews and Ann Jonas are both designers and illustrators, adding, "I started as a designer and most of my drawings are designs.

One of the illustrations from Leo the Late Bloomer *by Robert Kraus, published in* 1971. *The original is in full color.*

Children are design-minded. Design breaks it down to its simplest form."

For years now, Mr. Aruego has concentrated his designs and career on picture books. "Now I do not draw cartoons for magazines. I am involved with books and talks." He says that he enjoys interacting with people and is continually traveling around the country, speaking with schoolchildren as well as other writers and artists. What does he consider one of his major accomplishments? "I take particular pride in two books done nearly twenty years ago that are still around and popular." These two are *Whose Mouse Are You?* and *Leo the Late Bloomer*, both by Robert Kraus.

Another source of pride is his son, Juan. "All my books are dedicated to Juan. Now he is a journalist and working in Germany. He writes for a German newspaper, and works for magazines, too. He does special features. He comes home, so I have not visited him there."

Jose Aruego continues to create an enchanted world with playful animals, amusing backgrounds, shimmering colors, and memorable fables. Anyone can enter that world just by opening one of his books. In speaking of the future, he says, "This is what I will be doing for quite some time. Hopefully, people like my work. It is what I want to do." Mr. Aruego does not have to worry. People do like his work. They keep buying, borrowing, and reading his books, as each new one is published and as the older ones become classics.

Michael Chang

 In 1989, a full-page Reebok advertisement appeared in newspapers across the United States. It read: "Some kids go to Paris to study history, others go to make it." This ad was printed in celebration of Michael Chang's tennis victory in the French Open. At seventeen years old, Michael became the youngest male and the first American man in thirty-four years to win the French Open.

After winning the French Open, Michael Chang became a well-known celebrity almost overnight. He has been interviewed for magazines, newspapers, and television, including a guest appearance on "The Tonight Show." His success has made him a wealthy young man, both through his on-court winnings and product endorsements. Michael has not been swayed by the sudden fame and fortune. In fact, he says money means little to him, and that he spends his $100 monthly allowance very carefully.

Michael Chang, the younger of Joe and Betty Chang's two sons, was born on February 22, 1972, in Hoboken, New Jersey. Joe Chang left China during the revolution of 1948 and settled in Taiwan before coming to the United States in 1966. At the age of eleven, Betty Tung came to the United States from India where her father was a Chinese diplomat. While earning his graduate degree as a research chemist in New Jersey, Joe Chang met Betty, a New York college student, on a blind date. They married in 1966 and their first son, Carl, was born two years later.

A few years after Michael was born, Joe Chang took a job with the 3M Company in St. Paul, Minnesota. It was here that Joe Chang discovered an interest in tennis. To learn the game, Mr. Chang read books and magazines. He practiced almost daily until his wife suggested that he spend more time with his sons and teach them tennis, too. The Chang family enjoyed the sport so much that they decided to move to an area where they could play tennis all year-round. Joe Chang moved his family from St. Paul to La Costa, near San Diego, in California. Tuesday through Friday, Michael and Carl played practice games for an hour and a half (they took Mondays off), and played in tournaments every weekend. This routine helped the Chang boys work their way up in the tennis rankings of amateur players.

Michael Chang was six years old when he first started to play tennis. He won his first tournament in San Diego at the age of seven. At fifteen and a half, Michael won a match in the U.S. National Junior Championships, succeeding over many players who were two to three years older than he was. During this time, Michael had several tennis coaches, but he has said many times that the best trainer has always been his father. Through the years, Mr. Chang has recorded and gathered advice from each coach to help perfect Michael's tennis technique.

When Michael was a tenth grader, his tennis career was well under way but began to have an impact on his schooling. With all the traveling, training, and tournaments, Michael attended high school on an average of two days a week. According to his counselor at Placentia High School, located about thirty miles east of Los Angeles, Michael made good grades but his tennis schedule and decision to turn pro in February, 1988, caused him to leave school. According to Michael's parents, there were many pros and cons to this decision. On the one hand, they felt that their son was mature enough to handle the pressures of the pro tour. On the other hand, the family did not have the finances to pay for all the airline tickets, hotels, and equipment necessary to compete on the pro circuit. A large endorsement contract was offered by Reebok to sixteen-year-old Michael, which made it possible for him to turn professional. Before turning his full-time attention to the pro tennis schedule, Michael earned his high school G.E.D. (General Educational Development) certificate.

Michael does not feel that he has missed out on too much by dropping out of high school, and is confident he will eventually attend college to continue his education after tennis. In deciding on a tennis career at an early age, Michael understands that he also made a choice that would make his life very different from most other people. Because of his busy schedule, he is not able to do many of the things that other teen-agers do, such as dating, driving, or "hanging out" with friends. Instead, these experiences have been replaced by traveling around the world and meeting people from many different countries.

Each year, Michael and most other professional players participate in four major tennis tournaments. These tournaments, called the "Grand Slam" events, are the most important ones to the players and most well-known to the fans. They are held in different countries around the world: Australia—the Australian Open; France—the French Open; England—Wimbledon; and in America—the U.S. Open. Michael has made tennis history by being the youngest to accomplish high honors in almost all of these main events. In 1987, when Michael was fifteen, he was the youngest to win a U.S. Open match. The following year, he advanced far enough in the Wimbledon match to become the youngest player in sixty years to play on the prestigious Centre Court. In 1989, Michael claimed his historic French Open victory, where he became the tournament's youngest male winner in history and the first U.S. man to triumph since 1955.

The two-week French Open is played in Paris. The courts are made of red clay and topped with a layer of crushed red brick. As the ball hits this clay surface it slows down, giving players more time to get to each shot

Michael Chang, champion of the French Open, Paris, 1989

and return it. Tennis courts with hard or grass surfaces give more speed to the ball as it bounces, making it easier for players to serve "aces," which are unreturnable serves, and "clean winners," a shot a player cannot reach in time to return. Aces and clean winners both help shorten the length of matches. Points are scored much faster than on clay courts. On clay, players need to have strong legs to be able to endure matches that can last longer than five hours.

Michael credits his historic win to mental toughness, good strategy, and strong legs. During his rise in the tennis ranks, Michael almost always competed against older, stronger opponents. He has said that playing tough opponents has taught him to deal better with the tough situations of today. In the 1989 French Open, Michael Chang played the semifinal match against the No. 1 player in the world, Ivan Lendl, of Czechoslovakia. Michael's father had work to get back to at home in California and, thinking his son was such an underdog, did not stay to watch the match. After a grueling five-hour match, during which Michael suffered and played with severe leg cramps, Chang defeated Lendl in an emotional and courageous finish. In reflecting on this memorable match, Michael has said that he was trying to break Lendl's mental concentration to make up for the physical disadvantage created by his leg cramps. Following the semifinal match against Lendl, Michael Chang defeated Stefan Edberg of Sweden, ranked No. 3 in the world, to gain the French Open title.

By the end of 1989, Michael Chang had earned over

$680,000 in tournament winnings and became the youngest player to rank in the men's tennis "Top Five" in the world. One of his first matches as the No. 5 ranked player in the world was to take place in the $650,000 Stakes Match in Palm Coast, Florida. While practicing for this tournament, Michael suffered a freak injury. As he ran to return a shot, his strong twisting motion caused a stress fracture where the ball of the hip joint connects with the hip socket. Usually this type of injury occurs in contact sports, such as football, and is uncommon to tennis players. Rest and hip muscle exercises were prescribed to regain strength in this area.

Although the hip injury was a temporary setback, many experts feel that Michael is still about five years away from reaching his peak performance level. Michael Chang returned to championship tennis in Chicago and Toronto, Canada, when he captured the Volvo (March, 1990) and Player's International (July, 1990) tournament titles. In September of 1990, Michael Chang won a key semifinal match that advanced the United States team to the Davis Cup finals for the first time since 1984. The team became Davis Cup champions in late December. Michael has taken part in a rigorous training program similar to strenuous tournament schedules to build his endurance and to prevent his hip injury from reoccurring. Each day of nontournament weeks, Chang practices particular tennis strokes, his serve, and game strategy for about two hours. Then he runs three miles before playing in a practice match in the afternoon.

Michael Chang knows that he will not be able to win

*Michael Chang hitting a backhand at the 1990 Volvo
Tournament in Chicago*

all the time, and considers tournament defeats as well as
victories in preparing himself mentally. His religious
beliefs and his parents' support help to strengthen his
mental game. Some might call him humble; Michael feels
he is realistic. "I know that if I can stay on the court
long enough, I can figure out what I have to do to beat
most players," he has said. That mental toughness is one
of Michael Chang's strongest assets. It is anchored in his
family and his faith. Michael is a devout Christian, which
he says serves to calm him during tight situations.

Support also comes through Joe Chang's coaching and direction of his son's tennis career. Michael's comforts are attended to by his mother, Betty, with home-cooked meals on the road and her careful management of the many scheduling details involved on the pro tennis tour. This support system, along with Michael's mental strength, have given him the added edge in this sport. Tennis pros John McEnroe and Arthur Ashe have both commented on how Michael Chang's strong mental sense and intuition have given him the composure usually seen in older, more experienced players.

When Michael is not practicing, playing, or mentally preparing for a tennis match, he can be found in Placentia, California, where he lives with his parents. Michael is a fishing enthusiast and, in particular, enjoys fishing for freshwater bass. Keeping mentally and physically fit is important to Michael, especially in a career that includes weekly trips covering thousands of miles and facing tennis serves that seem to come toward him at 1,000 miles per hour.

In the coming years Michael Chang will put in many hours of hard work to reach his goal of bringing each technical part of his tennis game to the highest possible level he can achieve. If he is successful, with all the other qualities he has going for him, Michael Chang will certainly have a chance at carving a very special place for himself in tennis history.

When asked to share his recipe for success, Michael Chang replied, "Be sure that you really enjoy what you're doing; build on the talents given to you and work on your weaknesses. There are no shortcuts to life; hard work is the only way to go. Strive to be the best you can be and remember that when you try your best, you can't ask any more from yourself and people can't ask any more from you."

Michael Chang in a casual moment

Connie Chung

Connie Chung is a "nuclear reactor of energy!" This is the term Dan Rather once used to describe this powerful and important news anchorperson. Connie Chung has been ready to tackle new and bigger challenges throughout her career. In order to do this, she has moved from the East Coast to the West Coast and then back to the East Coast again. She has switched from a local Washington, D.C., station (WTTG) to CBS News to a local CBS station to NBC News and has now returned to CBS News. During one move, she took a chance and reportedly accepted a cut in salary in order to try new areas of broadcasting. Connie's risk-taking and willingness to undertake almost any news assignment has been rewarded. She is one of the highest-paid, most-popular, and sought-after female broadcast journalists in the nation.

Constance Yu-hwa Chung was born in Washington, D.C., on August 20, 1946, the youngest of ten children. Five of the Chungs' children died in China during wartime when it was difficult to get medical attention. Her father, William Ling Chung, was a diplomat in Chiang Kai-shek's government. He moved his wife and Connie's four older sisters from China to Washington in 1945 where he began working for the Chinese Embassy and later for the United Nations. Connie was the only child born in the United States.

As a youngster, Connie was very quiet, especially around her four older sisters. Connie has recalled a time when she cried all the way home after her elementary schoolteacher commented on her report card that she spoke too softly. However, in high school she became more actively involved through student government. Growing up in the nation's capital, she developed an interest in government activities.

Beginning her college years as a biology major at the University of Maryland, Connie did not lose her attraction to politics. She worked one summer writing speeches and press releases for a New York Congressman, and then changed her major from biology to journalism. Her next move was as a copy person for a Washington, D.C., television station, WTTG. After graduation, she became a secretary in the WTTG news department, advancing to newswriter and to on-air reporter.

In the early 1970s, the Federal Communications Commission (FCC) urged television networks to open their doors to women and minorities. Connie was hired by CBS

News, along with three other women reporters, and soon earned a reputation for being tenacious and hard-working. She approached her stories with enthusiasm and determination, covering key political figures in the news. She covered George McGovern's 1972 campaign for President. During Watergate, she persisted in covering the stories of the main characters, standing outside their homes as they picked up the morning newspaper, just to have the opportunity to ask a few questions on-camera.

Connie joined the Los Angeles CBS station as co-anchor in 1976. She gained in popularity for her energetic telecasts resulting in local news ratings rising from third to second place. She became one of the highest-paid local news anchors in the country. Her broadcasting skills and personable style emerged during this time. She strove for perfection on-camera, but soon learned to cope with unexpected events during live telecasts. Connie has recalled one broadcast where the chain on her watch got stuck on her blouse microphone just as she was to open the news. With her hand caught near her throat, Connie said, "Good evening" to her television viewers. In order to make Connie feel better, her co-anchor, Jess Marlow, also held his hand to his chest and said, "In other news . . ."

In 1983, Connie left local news and switched over to NBC Network News, moving back to the East Coast. Connie welcomed the challenge of her new job. She worked long, hard days, waking up at three o'clock in the morning to prepare for the "NBC News at Sunrise" from 6:30–7:00 A.M., Monday through Friday. She would sleep about three hours at night and then three hours in the afternoon before appearing on the "NBC Nightly News" or the "NBC News Digest" at 9:00 or 10:00 P.M. On Saturdays, she anchored the network's Saturday evening news.

Even though her hours were long, Connie was profiting in other areas. She was given the opportunity to anchor special shows during prime time and gained more nationwide exposure. Much of her time was spent doing documentaries or special informative programs.

Connie Chung co-anchored NBC's weekly news magazine program with Roger Mudd. As the show and Connie gained in popularity, she gave up anchoring "NBC News at Sunrise" to devote more time to the news magazine. Among the topics covered by the weekly program were automobile safety and advances in genetic engineering.

In 1987, NBC televised live reports from Beijing and other cities in China. Ms. Chung visited China for the first time as part of the news team. Since she speaks Chinese, Connie was able to speak directly to many of the Chinese citizens. Prior to this trip, she made use of her Chinese language ability when preparing news stories on visiting Chinese diplomats, gymnasts, or Ping-Pong players. She interviewed relatives that she had never met before, who told of their experiences during the war and Cultural Revolution. She also learned about modern China and how her relatives became the people they are today—an architect, a college professor, and an accountant. This very special reporting assignment brought Connie a special connection to her heritage.

By covering the 1984 and 1988 presidential elections,

Connie Chung again became a part of politics and government. She appeared on television to report on the progress of the Republican and Democratic candidates during each party's nominating conventions. In Atlanta, Connie also captured the big story of the day when she was the first to interview Jesse Jackson and, later, John F. Kennedy, Jr., at the Democratic convention.

In the following year, Connie Chung rejoined CBS News where she first started. In addition to anchoring the "CBS Evening News, Sunday Edition," she would have her own weekly show, "Saturday Night with Connie Chung." The show pioneered a different approach for broadcasting news stories. Actors and actresses played the roles of real people who are a part of actual news events. In her first show, the actor James Earl Jones played the part of Rev. Vernon Johns, a supporter of civil rights. In another show, actor Scott Wentworth played Terry Anderson, who was being held hostage in the Middle East. By presenting major news stories in this manner, Ms. Chung gave viewers a longer, more in-depth look at important historical events that could not be told as effectively any other way.

After a highly successful trial-run, Ms. Chung's news program moved to Monday nights as "Face to Face with Connie Chung," presenting a mix of news stories, investigative pieces, off-beat features, and interviews with important people in the news. For her broadcasts, Connie interviewed the likes of *Exxon Valdez* Captain Joseph Hazelwood and actor Marlon Brando, and reported on such stories as the bombing of the Pan Am Flight 103, the

"Saturday Night with Connie Chung"

Former Middle East hostages, Father Lawrence Jenco and David Jacobsen, are interviewed by Connie Chung on "Saturday Night with Connie Chung."

American hostages in Lebanon, and the unchecked powers of the Internal Revenue Service.

Connie Chung's professionalism and readiness to try novel ideas has often earned her special awards. She was named as Woman of the Year in 1975 by the *Ladies Home Journal*, and the Los Angeles Press Club recognized her television reporting as the best in 1977. Her report titled "Shot in Hollywood" earned her an Emmy Award from the National Academy of Television Arts and Sciences in

1987. She is also the recipient of a George Foster Peabody Award for a series of educational programs on the environment, and a U.S. Humane Society Certificate of Achievement for her reporting on the cruelties of seal harvesting.

Enjoying her career, Ms. Chung did not decide to marry until she was thirty-eight years old. In 1984, she married Maury Povich who is the anchor of the popular television program, "A Current Affair." The two first met when she was working at WTTG in Washington and Mr. Povich was a news anchor and talk-show host. Their careers took separate paths and they did not see each other again until they worked together in Los Angeles as co-anchors for KNXT News in 1977. Connie and Maury did not live in the same city until after they were married several years later. They accumulated many air miles to visit each other. At the time of their marriage, Ms. Chung was based in New York and her husband was in Washington, D.C. Finally, Mr. Povich moved to New York where he hosted "A Current Affair." Weekdays are spent in their apartment on Manhattan's West Side and weekends in a New Jersey home.

Currently, there are no women anchoring a week-night network news broadcast on their own. Ms. Chung had once commented that a woman anchor in this position might not happen in her lifetime, but that a woman co-anchor was a possibility. It was several years ago that Dan Rather called Connie Chung a "nuclear reactor of energy." Co-workers say she is still one of the hardest-working journalists in the business.

Myung-Whun Chung

 The character Hector was already dead, so he was not to move an inch as debris fell unexpectedly onto the stage and narrowly missed him. Some of the new theater's machinery did not work and had to be powered by hand. The scene was March 17, 1990, opening night at the new Opera de la Bastille in Paris, France. The problems described were rather minor, though, when compared to the struggle it took to get the new opera created, built, and staffed. People argued that a cost equaling $400 million was too much to spend when the city already had a gorgeous opera house.

The site of the new opera was where the legendary French prison, the Bastille, had stood before it was stormed and destroyed during the French Revolution. While historic, some said it was not in a fashionable area.

Others did not like the modern design of the new building. As the completion drew closer, yet another new administrator was hired to oversee the project. Five months later, with less than a year to the opening date, the adminstrator dismissed the world-famous conductor who headed the opera. The musical world was vigilant as these controversies unfolded, and initially surprised at the conductor, Myung-Whun Chung, who was chosen as a replacement. Mr. Chung did not have much experience in conducting opera. He was only thirty-seven, relatively young for such an important post. He had been born in South Korea, trained in the United States, and could not even speak French.

With so many difficulties and last-minute changes, not many expected the instant acclaim won by the Opera de la Bastille and Mr. Chung. Yet that March 17 performance of *Les Troyens* (*The Trojans*) by French composer Hector Berlioz, with a cast of hundreds and running nearly six hours, was a resounding success for the new opera company, its curving steel and glass theater, and its music director, Myung-Whun Chung.

Mr. Chung may have been fairly new to opera and to France, but he already had a long career in music and many experiences in international living. Myung-Whun Chung was born on January 22, 1953, in Seoul, South Korea, the sixth of seven children in his family. Four of the seven would become gifted musicians, and their parents did everything to help them. Korea had been divided after World War II. The Soviet Union occupied the northern portion, while the United States military was

Myung-Whun Chung

in the south. During the Korean War in the early 1950s, Communist North Korea invaded South Korea. The Chung family moved temporarily from Seoul, farther south to Pusan. They considered a large piano to be one of their most necessary possessions, and it was moved with them.

Mr. and Mrs. Chung both enjoyed classical music, and the children were exposed to composers such as Bach and Beethoven. One of Myung-Whun's older sisters, Myung-

Wha, played the cello. When Myung-Whun was four and just beginning to study the piano, Myung-Wha was only thirteen but already performing with the Seoul Philharmonic Orchestra. About the same time, another older sister, Kyung-Wha, performed the Mendelssohn violin concerto with that orchestra. She was nine at the time. Another sibling, Myung-So, became a flutist. By the time Myung-Whun Chung was seven, he made his piano debut with the Seoul Philharmonic. It is very unusual for children to perform with a major orchestra, but the Chungs were exceptional musicians. Myung-Whun has said he also liked sports, but he always took his music very seriously.

Mr. and Mrs. Chung were in business in Seoul. The family lived a comfortable life, and all the children were taught music as part of their education. The family's life began to change, however, as they realized that too many of the children were gifted. Kyung-Wha, the violinist, has recalled that it became difficult to try to train them all. Her parents were quite happy when she won a scholarship which would pay tuition at the Juilliard School in New York City. She was only twelve, but left home to study in the United States. Within a year, the family followed.

By the time Myung-Whun Chung was eight, his parents had decided that the best education for their children was in the United States. In late 1961, they left their established surroundings in Seoul and moved to Seattle, Washington. The Chungs ran a Korean restaurant where Mr. Chung was a cook and Mrs. Chung was a waitress.

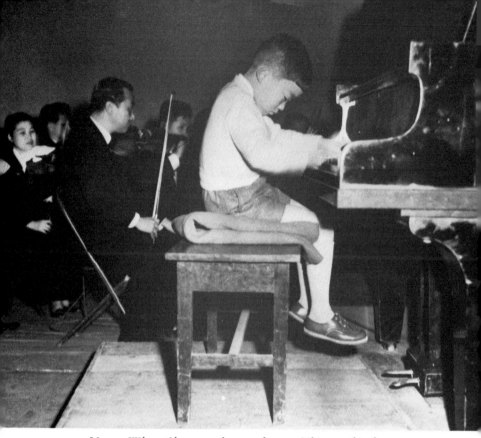

*Myung-Whun Chung at the age of seven. This was his first concert
as a pianist with the Seoul Philharmonic Orchestra.*

Daughters Kyung-Wha and Myung-Wha both attended
Juilliard in New York. Myung-Whun completed high
school in Seattle.

When he was eighteen, Myung-Whun Chung also
moved to New York City. He studied piano and conducting at the Mannes School of Music. When he was
twenty-one, he won second prize in the piano section of
the Tchaikovsky Competition in Moscow. This competition is one of the most important in the world and is

held only once every four years. After this success and a diploma from Mannes, Myung-Whun enrolled at Juilliard, primarily for conducting. Such training includes learning which instrumentalists play which parts in musical pieces, and how to have them perform together properly. During these years in New York, Myung-Whun met the woman he would later marry, and he became an American citizen. Professionally, he was appearing as a piano soloist with various orchestras, including the Los Angeles Philharmonic. He also was conducting youth symphonies and a Juilliard opera production. These talents and associations helped shape his career, even as its focus shifted.

By 1978, Myung-Whun Chung was only twenty-five, but he had already been performing for eighteen years. He was still uncertain whether he would become a full-time conductor when he was named Assistant Conductor of the Los Angeles Philharmonic Orchestra. His post began in October, 1978, under conductor Carlo Maria Giulini. He helped Mr. Giulini and guest conductors, and also had the opportunity to lead the orchestra. Within a few years, Myung-Whun Chung had risen to Associate Conductor, and he had also married. His wife's name is Sunyol.

The 1980s brought even more changes to Mr. Chung's career and family life. Myung-Whun decided to move to Europe to concentrate more on music. He felt that especially in the United States, much of a music director's time is devoted to administration, publicity, and fundraising, in addition to actual conducting. Less than ten years later, Mr. Chung would be performing all these duties as Music Director of the Bastille Opera, but in the early 1980s, he still wanted more pure musical experience. He also enjoyed the different cultures in Europe. Looking back, he thinks he benefited from conducting in different cities and feeling different attitudes toward certain music. He has said that conducting an opera by the Italian composer Verdi in Italy is not the same as conducting it elsewhere. In 1984, he took a post as the Music Director and Principal Conductor for the Radio Symphony Orchestra in Saarbrücken, West Germany. A few years later, he also added a position as a principal guest conductor in Italy. At the same time, he appeared as a guest conductor with major orchestras in many countries, including Germany, the Netherlands, France, Great Britain, Israel, and the United States. He also continued his piano and performed as part of the Chung Trio with sisters Kyung-Wha and Myung-Wha.

Professional life was very busy and filled with travel, but Myung-Whun Chung's routine changed dramatically as his family expanded. By 1985, the Chungs had three sons, Jin, Sun, and Min. Before they were born, Mr. Chung says he kept very late hours, as did many musicians. After the children arrived, he reversed his schedule in order to spend time with them. He went to bed and arose much earlier. He used the quiet time, before his sons awoke, to study. He tries to stay home on the evenings when he is not working. He does not have much free time, but likes to spend it with his family. When Mr. Chung's sons were younger, they often traveled with him as he performed in different cities. Once the boys began school, however, that became difficult. The Chungs have provided musical training for their boys, but so far Mr. Chung does not think they show professional promise. He has not encouraged them in musical careers because he knows such a life is not easy. He says that with extraordinary talent, a person can choose to become a musician or seek another career. Without such a gift, however, a person does not have a choice.

Myung-Whun Chung at the age of nineteen

With his post in Paris, Mr. Chung does not travel as much as in the past. In his contract with the Bastille Opera, he agreed to spend six months a year in Paris, but he will try to be there even more. He wants the stability. Before moving to Paris, he lived with his family in Rome, Italy, even though he was primarily working in Germany. He admits the reason he chose to reside in Italy was because cooking is his only real hobby. He says that he craves pasta and basically moved to Italy for its food.

Living in Italy provided Mr. Chung's beloved cuisine and also more experience in conducting opera. In 1987, Mr. Chung became Principal Guest Conductor of the Teatro Comunale in Florence, Italy. During his very first season in Florence, Mr. Chung won the Premio Abbiati, a prestigious operatic award. He had already debuted at the Metropolitan Opera in New York City, and he continued to conduct opera in many cities such as Monte Carlo, Monaco, and Geneva, Switzerland, and the one which would catapult him to fame, Paris. Prophetically, he even planned to conduct a production of *Les Troyens*, to be performed in Florence in 1991.

The Opera de la Bastille was eagerly anticipated ever since French President François Mitterrand had announced plans in 1982. The new Opera would be accessible to more people than the productions in the old, ornate theater. There was talk of giving as many as two hundred and fifty opera performances a year in the new theater, while the existing opera palace would be devoted to dance. The new structure would be ready for July 14, 1989, France's Bicentennial, a celebration of the two-

Myung-Whun Chung conducting a rehearsal for Les Troyens *at the Opera de la Bastille*

hundredth anniversary of the French Revolution. In organizing such a project, building the actual opera house was only one of many important factors. The opera company had to develop a repertory, a collection of operas it was prepared to perform. The opera productions had to be planned ahead because soloists are usually contracted for years in advance. An orchestra had to be chosen. Set designers, costumers, and lighting technicians had to be hired. The music director was often involved in these details.

From the beginning, there were controversies and problems. Disagreements between people at the top levels of the company were highly publicized, and in January of 1989, the then music director was dismissed. When he left, much of what he had planned was abandoned. Just two months before the Bicentennial, Mr. Chung was selected to replace him. The fast-approaching season had to be organized, once again from the beginning. The opening opera itself was even changed.

The massive building was not yet complete when it hosted a Bicentennial gala, as promised. World-famous opera stars such as Placido Domingo sang, while many international leaders such as President George Bush enjoyed the concert. Right after the festivities, construction workers resumed their jobs. Mr. Chung had not conducted this special event, but he prepared feverishly for the actual premiere of the new opera company, only seven months away.

The Opera de la Bastille officially opened with *Les Troyens*. The performance had its share of minor, first-night mishaps, but at the end of the long evening, Mr. Chung was swiftly praised in his new role. Within days, a French newspaper reported how the audience adopted the new company with ten minutes of applause and cheering. An American magazine called the production "triumphant." Almost overnight, the years of turmoil seemed to be over. Yet the hard work of developing one of the world's best opera companies was far from complete.

To the audience, Mr. Chung is seen as the conductor,

but his job involves much more. He will shape the quality and offerings of the opera company. He personally hears the auditions of many singers and musicians. He strives to improve the orchestra and chorus, which came from the old Paris opera, but he is also faced with the reality that the salaries paid by the French government are limited. He has tried to increase money available by getting recording and television broadcast contracts. He wants the repertory to expand and include older favorite operas by composers such as Verdi and Mozart, as well as lesser-known contemporary ones. Mr. Chung also wants to emphasize French opera, since the Bastille is the French national opera. Another part of his job is arranging co-productions of operas with other companies, such as La Scala in Milan, Italy.

Myung-Whun Chung views all this responsibility as a challenge. He works sixteen hours a day in one of the world's most visible music posts. He is anxious to turn from his administrative duties and concentrate more on the musical portion of his position, but he knows that organizing an opera will take years. In the meantime, he is prepared to remain stationed in Paris for awhile. He says that wherever his family is, he feels at home, and he is continually improving his French.

Wendy Lee Gramm

Dr. Wendy Lee Gramm wanted the job concerning frozen pork bellies, live cattle, cotton, and cocoa, but she was not a farmer or in the grocery supply business. The position also covered the Japanese yen, crude oil, and gold. Dr. Gramm was an economist, and on February 3, 1988, at 9:00 A.M., she stepped before the U.S. Senate Agriculture Committee, ready to be questioned about her selection as Chairman of the Commodity Futures Trading Commission. The hearing lasted two and a half hours. The testimony was almost entirely about her professional qualifications and views, although there were also references to her background and personal life. It was mentioned that her grandfathers came from Korea to work in the Hawaiian sugar fields. Her submitted resume included a school PTA membership. It was noted that she was married to a senator from Texas, Phil Gramm. Two weeks after that hearing, Dr. Gramm was approved by a voice vote in the full Senate, and she took the job.

Growing up, Wendy Gramm never expected to be an economist or work in the government. She had grown up in Hawaii, but chose to attend college in distant Massachusetts. She did not expect to marry and have two children within five years of finishing her Ph.D. She had a permanent university position in Texas, but abruptly moved to Washington, D.C., with her husband. Dr. Gramm has always been open to new experiences and weighed the "costs and benefits" of each situation. Her flexibility and hard work have shaped her life and career. She also credits the values and examples of her parents and grandparents.

Wendy Lee Gramm was born on January 10, 1945, in Waialua on the island of Oahu, Hawaii. She was the third girl for Angeline and Joshua Lee, and a younger brother came later. Her mother was a librarian, and her father worked for the Waialua Sugar Company. Both sets of her grandparents were originally from Korea, but they had come to Hawaii many years earlier.

"My grandfathers came to work in the sugarcane fields of Hawaii. They were contract laborers, which means that they contracted for passage over, and then agreed to work until they paid it off. They came about the beginning of the twentieth century. There were a fair number of Koreans, but Koreans were still a small proportion of the Hawaiian population as a whole. My mother's father sent back to Korea for a 'picture bride.' My grandmother sent

Wendy Lee Gramm visiting the Chicago Mercantile Exchange,
1988

a picture and the bachelor in Hawaii, my grandfather,
agreed that she was the one he wanted." He worked on
the plantations for a few years to fulfill his commitment.
"He then became a construction worker and helped build
some of the major old structures in Hawaii." She continues "My mother's parents wanted to learn English and
become proficient. My mother can understand a little bit
of Korean, but the language did not get passed on. She
is a wonderful cook, though, and the food did get passed
on!"

On her father's side, her grandmother came to Hawaii
as a young child, and her grandfather worked for many

years on the sugar plantations. In the early 1950s, they helped South Korea. "When the Korean War broke out, and the Communists were flooding in, my grandparents went back to Korea and volunteered. After the war, my grandmother got a commendation for keeping the telephone exchange open during bombing, and my grandfather for driving people around by taxi. He was wounded. They were commended by the Korean government for their efforts in helping to keep Korea free." They returned to Hawaii to live, with occasional visits to Korea.

Wendy Gramm says that although her father spoke Korean when she was young, his family also learned English. He was the second of nine children, was graduated from high school during the economic depression of the 1930s, but still left the islands for college. "In those days, you got on the boat, went off to college, and you did not know if you were going to come back for years. He went to Tri-State College in Angola, Indiana, and had jobs to work his way through college." To earn room and board, he did yard work. He was so serious about keeping one job he had in a restaurant that he "raced" a dishwasher to prove he was actually faster.

After her father earned his degree in engineering, he went back to Waialua to the same sugar company where his own father had been a contract laborer. He worked hard and had many promotions. Wendy Lee Gramm smiles. "He ended up being a vice-president of the company and was the first Asian to hold a managerial position in the company."

Wendy Lee and her family lived close to the sugar company, "out in the country. Those years, growing up was very casual and very much outside. We did not have to wear shoes until, I think, we were in the fifth grade. We could go barefoot to school, if we wanted to, until then. I took ballet, modern dance, and piano, and had a very normal type of childhood. This was a small town and these were not fancy classes, though. We wore socks to do turns. We did not buy toe shoes!

"When I was in grade school, I do not think I had a favorite subject. I had a favorite doll, maybe, but not a favorite subject. I enjoyed them all. My favorite books were biographies and biographical novels. Then, of course, there were all the Wilder books, those 'Little House' books, and *A Tree Grows in Brooklyn*."

In 1957, half a world away, the Soviet Union launched the satellite called Sputnik. Dr. Gramm says this one event probably triggered her future direction and career, as U.S. schools responded. "When I was in eighth grade, Sputnik went up, and all of a sudden, everybody looked around and asked, 'Do we have enough scientists and engineers?' So, our class started accelerating programs, taking alegbra in the eighth grade. By the time I was a senior, I took calculus and even some statistics. I took the Advanced Placement exam, went to Wellesley, and was going to be a math major. I found math in college hard and boring, but I had taken a lot of math, so I switched to economics. I chose economics because it was close to business and I knew that I could use my math."

Wendy had received an academic scholarship at Wellesley College after graduating from high school.

Wellesley, in often frigid and snowy Massachusetts, was a big adjustment for her. She was accustomed to wearing sandals and did not even own a wool dress. She majored in economics and also continued a favorite activity. "I auditioned and got into the Wellesley dance group. In college, it really was an important extracurricular activity. Instead of being totally focused on books, I was able to excel, to some extent, in something other than schoolwork."

After graduating from college in 1966, Wendy traded one cold location for another. She attended graduate school at Northwestern University in Evanston, Illinois, near Chicago. She says that she soon realized there were not many women studying economics. Her classes at Wellesley had been filled with other women, but it was a women's college. At co-ed Northwestern, however, she was surprised that women were only a small percentage of the economics program. Wendy enjoyed her studies and completed her degree with research on married women in the labor supply.

Wendy Lee received her Ph.D. from Northwestern in 1971, and was recruited for jobs. She interviewed for a position as an Assistant Professor of Economics at Texas A&M University. "I really liked to do research and papers. I decided academics would be good because you teach and do research." Dr. William Philip Gramm, already an economics professor at Texas A&M, first met Wendy Lee at that interview. He was one of several faculty members present, although he was not on the interview committee. He was very impressed by Wendy's qualifications, and also by her personality. After she left the session, he told a colleague he would marry her. Dr. Wendy Lee accepted the position at Texas A&M because she was impressed with the school and its economics department. She was not initially impressed by Dr. Phil Gramm. Soon after she arrived on the College Station, Texas, campus, however, the two began dating. They were married just three months later. She was twenty-five and he was twenty-eight.

While both Dr. Gramms were teaching at Texas A&M, their family grew. Marshall Kenneth was born in 1973, and Jefferson Philip in 1975. "I knew that if I had children it would be really hard in a lot of ways, but I did not want to miss the experience and it has been great fun," Wendy Gramm says. Raising children was made a bit easier by a flexible academic schedule.

Wendy Gramm was promoted to Associate Professor and received tenure, which meant her position was permanent. She continued to teach, do research, and publish her results. She was also Director of Undergraduate Programs in the economics department, advising students and preparing teaching schedules.

The Gramms were both still at Texas A&M when Phil Gramm, with Wendy's support, decided to challenge U.S. Senator Lloyd Bentsen of Texas in the 1976 Democratic primary for the U.S. Senate. Phil Gramm lost that race, but ran for another political office in 1978. Both Phil and Wendy campaigned hard. He was elected to the U.S. House of Representatives, and the family's life abruptly changed. Wendy Gramm truly enjoyed her position at Texas A&M, but "You are always giving up

Senator Phil Gramm, Dr. Wendy Gramm, sons Jefferson and Marshall in front of a statue of Sam Houston at the U.S. Capitol, 1989

something every time you do something else. When my husband decided to run for Congress, I decided that I was going to work as hard as I could, but I knew that if he won, we were going to have to move to Washington. College Station is wonderful, but you cannot always be worried about what you are missing back home."

Phil Gramm was elected in November, 1978, and had to be in Washington just two months later for the start of the new Congress, a move that also affected Wendy Gramm's career. She recounts, "I did not really have time to look at academics. You win in November, you move in January, and you certainly do not make plans about moving beforehand. You only think about an election! I found a job not in government, not in academics, but in a 'think tank.' " Dr. Wendy Gramm was hired by the Institute for Defense Analyses, a research center that works on federal contracts, and she had "top secret clearance."

Representative Phil Gramm was reelected in 1980. Wendy Gramm was in Washington, but not particularly eager to work for the government and be part of such a large system of departments. She was recruited by James Miller III, Chairman of the Federal Trade Commission (FTC) and a former colleague at Texas A&M, and after awhile, she changed her mind. "I thought, 'If I am in Washington, and I am an economist dealing with regulatory issues, I should at least spend a little time in government, and what better time for trying it out than now?' I went to work in the FTC and found it very satisfying, so I stayed."

Dr. Gramm began with the FTC in March, 1982, as the Assistant Director in its Division of Consumer Protection. The following year, she rose to be Director of its Bureau of Economics. She headed a staff of about 150, including ninety Ph.D.'s. Meanwhile, Representative Phil Gramm had been reelected again in November of 1982, but early in 1983, he switched political parties. He wanted to make sure the voters approved, so he resigned his Congressional seat and re-ran as a Republican in a special election. He won. The following year, 1984, he decided to try for the U.S. Senate once again, but this time as a Republican. Wendy had become a Republican, too.

In August, 1984, Wendy Gramm resigned her position to campaign for her husband's election. She returned to Texas, shaking hands at supermarkets and giving speeches. Toward the end of the campaign, her parents came from Hawaii to stay with the boys in Washington. Phil Gramm won and joined his old opponent, Senator Lloyd Bentsen, in representing Texas in the U.S. Senate. Right after the election, Wendy agreed to resume her same position with the FTC, but within a year she took another government position.

In October, 1985, she became the Administrator of the Office of Information and Regulatory Affairs in the Office of Management and Budget (OMB). She worked on issues such as the regulation of asbestos, a dangerous fiber, in the workplace. She was also concerned with any proposed changes in federal regulations and forms which collected data, such as the census. "When I was at OMB, reviewing all the paperwork, that was a fascinating job. I got to work with President George Bush when he was Vice-President. Then the White House asked me to take this job," she said, referring to her position as Chairman of the Commodity Futures Trading Commission. President Ronald Reagan had called Dr. Gramm his "favorite economist." She had a reputation for wanting as little governmental regulation as possible, and was the Executive Director of the Presidential Task Force on Regulatory Relief.

Wendy Gramm had worked at OMB for two years when she was mentioned in the press as a possible Secretary of Transportation. Elizabeth Dole was resigning that position to help her husband, Sen. Robert Dole, run for President. Dr. Gramm did not succeed Secretary Dole, but on December 3, 1987, she was officially selected by President Reagan to chair the Commodity Futures Trading Commission.

The selection of Chairman has to have the consent of the U.S. Senate, after a hearing by the Senate's Agriculture Committee. Wendy Gramm was accompanied to that hearing by two senators who were not on the committee, but appearing as witnesses on her behalf. Senator Daniel Inouye of Hawaii listed the accomplishments of the native of his state, and Senator Lloyd Bentsen of Texas also praised her. It was noted that she really had the support of both senators from Texas, since Phil Gramm was the other one.

Dr. Wendy Gramm was approved by the Senate and then sworn in as Chairman of the CFTC on February 22, 1988. The CFTC was created by Congress in 1974, and has the authority to regulate commodity futures and options trading. The Commission regulates the actions of nearly 400 commodity brokerage firms, over 55,000 salespeople, and over 7,500 floor brokers. The responsibilities of the CFTC include making sure the markets are competitive, efficient, and honest, and protecting market customers. Futures contracts are commitments, at a specific price and future date, to buy or sell commodities, such as the frozen pork bellies and cotton. Financial instruments, such as Japanese yen and U.S. Treasury Bonds, are also included. Futures options give the right, but not the obligation, to buy or sell futures contracts. Very few futures trades actually involve the delivery of the commodity. The frozen turkeys, live hogs, unleaded gasoline, lumber, or silver are rarely seen by the customers who buy and sell on paper before the delivery date. The CFTC licenses exchanges, such as the Chicago Mercantile Exchange, for the legal buying and selling of futures contracts. The prices of futures contracts are established in open auctions on these authorized exchanges.

While Dr. Gramm has been Chairman of the CFTC, it has cooperated with the FBI in action against dishonesty, has approved changes aimed at helping during a market crash, and also approved a new electronic trading system. She says, "This job is fascinating because it is an international marketplace, with the most innovative, cutting-edge financial market issues." Dr. Gramm was nominated for a second term as Chairman, which the Senate Agriculture Committee approved in August, 1990.

The Gramm family after a deer hunt

Wendy Gramm's job is very demanding, but she still makes sure she has time with her family. "I like to be with the children in the morning. I will stay at home until they go to school, and I enjoy driving them." Wendy even tries to include her sons in fitness routines, such as jogging, instead of exercising without them. She says that she and her husband do not go out very much at night. "We do have plenty of events we have to attend, but we do not accept many dinner invitations because we would rather be home with the children. We go for some weekends out of town with the boys, but it is very family oriented. They are getting really big and are going to be gone soon, and there will be plenty of time to do other things then. Skiing is a good family activity. I get to go hunting, floating down the Colorado River in a raft, and climbing through the Grand Canyon. We have gone to London and Berlin, and showed the children the Berlin Wall before it came down. We go to Hawaii to play on the beach." Wendy Gramm is also pleased that the boys have accompanied Senator Gramm on some of his regular trips back to Texas. "During the summer, there is a break, and my husband will have a packed schedule, eight places a day. For years now, he has taken the boys for a week or so and they travel with him. They have enjoyed that." The entire family also goes to Texas for some A&M football games.

"It is always a good perspective to have children," she says, reflecting on the balance of her life. "We do a lot of fun things with them. It is a good excuse for me to get back on roller coasters!"

Daniel K. Inouye

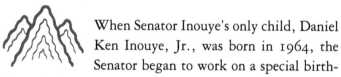 When Senator Inouye's only child, Daniel Ken Inouye, Jr., was born in 1964, the Senator began to work on a special birthday gift for him. Three years later, Senator Inouye's autobiography, *Journey to Washington*, was published. Senator Inouye wanted his son to know about his heritage and to understand everything about his father's life that led him to make the journey to Washington.

Daniel Ken Inouye was born on September 7, 1924, in Honolulu, Hawaii, the eldest son of the four children of Hyotaro and Kame Inouye. His father, Hyotaro, came to Hawaii from Japan with his parents when he was just four years old. Hyotaro attended Japanese and English schools in Hawaii while his father worked twelve-hour days on the Hawaiian sugar plantations, earning just ten dollars a month. Hyotaro met and married Kame Imanaga, an orphan adopted by the Methodist minister that their son Daniel was later named after. They settled on Queen Emma Street in a small Japanese ghetto in Honolulu. Their first son, Daniel, was born about a year later. Dan's father worked hard as a clerk in the jewelry section of a major department store, but finances were limited. To help save money, shoes were bought two sizes too big and stuffed with paper until the children grew into them. This did not bother Dan because Hawaii was always warm and he would rather go barefoot!

"I was too young to realize how underprivileged I was, and I enjoyed every moment of my childhood. There was always enough to eat in our house—although sometimes barely—but even more important, there was a conviction that opportunity awaited those who had the heart and strength to pursue it."

Young Dan grew up with a blending of Japanese and American cultures. He spoke Japanese before he learned to speak English. He attended public school and every afternoon he went to a Japanese school for an additional two hours. There he learned Japanese history and customs, as well as reading and writing in Japanese. When Dan was twelve years old he took a test to measure how well he spoke English. This test was given to all students at this age who had learned English as a second language. The students who passed this difficult test were allowed to attend English Standard schools. These public schools had the best buildings, playgrounds, libraries, and teachers. Dan was not admitted to an English Standard school. Even though his education continued in the public school

Daniel Inouye with sister and brothers in Hawaii, 1934. Left to right: Daniel, age ten; Mae Masako, age seven; John, age four; Robert, age two.

with mostly Asian students who did not pass the English language test, he was determined to become a surgeon. He read books on medicine and took first aid courses from the Red Cross to learn how to care for ill or injured people.

When Dan was not studying, he had several hobbies that he enjoyed. He collected postage stamps, raised homing pigeons and tropical fish, built crystal radio sets, experimented with chemistry sets, and played the piano and saxophone. To earn pocket money for these hobbies and other activities, Dan mowed lawns, gave haircuts to his friends, and parked cars at Honolulu Stadium. As the eldest son, Dan watched over and baby-sat his younger siblings. Living near the beach, he went spear fishing and surfing all year around. One of his favorite ways to earn money was when he was hired by tourists at the beachfront hotels to teach them how to surf the big Hawaiian waves.

Dan was a senior at McKinley High School when Pearl Harbor was attacked by the Japanese on December 7, 1941. "It was going to be a beautiful day. Already the sun had burned off the morning haze over Honolulu and, although there were clouds over the mountains, the sky was blue," he recalled of that fateful morning. Standing outside the house with his father, Dan could see Japanese dive bombers and black puffs of antiaircraft smoke from the U.S. Pacific Fleet anchored in Pearl Harbor.

The secretary of the Red Cross station where Dan had been teaching first aid ordered him to report immediately to help care for the injured. Dan worked day and night as head of a first aid litter team, sleeping whenever he could. There was so much to do to care for the injured that a week passed before he was able to return home. After the initial emergency was over, young Dan was given a regular shift to work from six in the evening to six in the morning. He was still a student and attended his high school classes in the morning, came home in the afternoon, slept until 5:30 P.M., and then left for the aid station to train new volunteers and to teach first aid to high school students.

Dan and other Americans of Japanese descent felt

ashamed at what Japan had done. When Hawaii became
a territory of the United States in 1900, its people became
American citizens and pledged allegiance to the United
States. But now, Americans of Japanese ancestry became
targets of suspicion and resentment. At the beginning of
the war, Japanese Americans were discharged from Hawaii's National Guard and were not allowed to enlist in
the armed forces. Young Japanese-American men wanting
to prove their loyalty by joining the United States Army
were not granted the opportunity.

Enrolled in premedical courses at the University of
Hawaii, eighteen-year-old Dan continued to pursue his
desire to become a doctor. However, the U.S. policy
changed and the army decided to accept Japanese-American volunteers to form a combat team to fight in the
front lines. Dan immediately volunteered to join the
442nd Infantry Regimental Combat Team and, after
completing very difficult training, was shipped over to
Italy. There he fought the Germans and Italians, who
sided with Japan in World War II.

The 442nd Combat Team was made up of Nisei, men
who were born in America to parents who moved here
from Japan. This unit is remembered for helping to win
one of the most famous battles of the war, the battle to
set free "The Lost Battalion." In this battle, the 442nd
rescued almost 1,000 soldiers of the 141st Infantry unit
who were surrounded by Germans and almost out of
ammunition and supplies. The courageous men of the
442nd were also nicknamed the "Go for Broke" Combat
Team. "It meant giving everything we had . . ." Dan

Daniel Inouye returning home from the war, shown with his father in Honolulu, Hawaii, 1945

Inouye explained. In 1951, MGM made a movie about the many contributions of the 442nd unit called *Go for Broke!* Van Johnson and Lane Nakano starred in this movie.

In April, 1945, Dan led his men up a heavily, German-defended hill. They shouted their battle cry, "Go for Broke!" Lt. Dan Inouye was struck by several bullets, but he continued to advance until his men were able to take the hill. Finally, his right arm was shattered by a German rifle grenade, yet he used his left hand to continue fighting. Just a few weeks later, the war in Italy was over.

Doctors could not save Dan Inouye's right arm. "Of

course, the arm had to come off. It wasn't an emotionally big deal for me. I knew it had to be done and had stopped thinking of it as belonging to me." He spent over a year and a half learning to live with one arm. By the time he was ready to leave the hospital, he could write, tie his shoelaces, play the piano, drive a car, use a knife and fork with only his left hand.

When Dan Inouye was reunited with his family in Hawaii, he was a Captain decorated with the Distinguished Service Cross (the second highest award for military bravery), Bronze Star, Purple Heart with two oak leaf clusters, and twelve other medals and citations.

With the loss of his right arm, Dan Inouye could not become a surgeon. However, he would not let his handicap get in the way of a career. He decided to go to law school and began prelaw courses at the University of Hawaii. There he met his wife, Margaret Awamura, who was teaching at the university.

"I proposed on our second date. It was December 6, 1947. I know, because we have celebrated the occasion together ever since. Of course, because we were Nisei, it wasn't as simple as all that. As soon as I informed my parents, they began to arrange things in the Japanese way. Tradition calls for *nakoudos*, go-betweens, who represent the families of the prospective bride and groom to settle the terms of the marriage." During an evening meeting between each family's go-between, parents, Dan, and Margaret, gifts of rice, sake, and fish were exchanged. The go-betweens also presented Dan's and Margaret's best qualities to each family. Finally, "The *nakoudos* consulted

Senator Inouye questioning Oliver North during the Iran-Contra hearings, Senate chambers, 1987

briefly with their clients, then recommended that the marriage be approved. At last, Maggie and I were engaged—officially!"

After completing his Bachelor of Arts degree in 1950, Dan left Hawaii and attended George Washington University Law School in Washington, D.C. He felt that this was the best place to see politics in action and to learn how laws are made. Dan became involved with the Democratic National Committee and gained many first-hand political experiences. He graduated from law school and began his first job as Deputy Public Prosecutor for the city and county of Honolulu.

Dan Inouye became very active in politics after returning from the war. At this time, Hawaii was still an

American territory. The people in Hawaii could send Democratic or Republican representatives to the United States Congress, but they were not given voting power. A governor who was appointed by the President ruled the Hawaiian Islands. Dan Inouye spent much of his time helping to rebuild the strength of the Democratic party of Hawaii. With the "Go for Broke" spirit, he opposed the powerful Republican candidate and was elected to the Territorial House of Representatives and became Territorial Majority Leader at the age of thirty. Four years later he was elected to the Territorial Senate.

In 1959, Hawaii became our 50th state. A new star was added to the flag, and Representatives and Senators would be sent for the first time to the U.S. Congress with full voting rights. Dan Inouye was overwhelmingly elected to hold Hawaii's first seat in the United States House of Representatives and at the same time became the first Japanese American to serve in Congress. In 1962, with 70 percent of the votes, he was elected to serve a six-year term as Senator. Since then, he has been successfully reelected to the Senate each term.

Dan Inouye began his long and distinguished career as a supporter of the civil rights movement. He was selected to deliver the important Keynote Address at the Democratic National Convention in 1968. He spoke about a better understanding between people of different races and working together to bring about change. As a member of the Senate Watergate Committee, he gained national respect and popularity with his skillful questioning of key witnesses. Because Dan Inouye proved his leadership abilities during the Watergate hearings, he

Senator Inouye in front of flag with "Go for Broke"
slogan, 1989

was appointed as the first chairman of the Senate Select
Committee on Intelligence in 1976.

After serving on the Select Committee on Intelligence
for eight years, Senator Inouye became chairman of a
group studying U.S. involvement in Central America.
With his Watergate experience and his knowledge of
Central America, the Senator was appointed to direct the

Iran-Contra public hearings in 1987. This committee investigated the secret sales of weapons by the government to help Iran and the Nicaraguan opposition army.

Currently, Dan Inouye is responsible for four committees: the Select Committee on Indian Affairs, the Appropriations Subcommittee on Defense, the Commerce Subcommittee on Communications, and the Senate Democratic Steering Committee.

The Senator and his wife have two homes, one in Bethesda, Maryland, and the other in Honolulu, Hawaii. His Washington, D.C., office is easy to recognize because it is decorated with tropical plants, fish tanks, and Hawaiian carvings, paintings, and leis. When relaxing, Senator Inouye enjoys gardening and playing one-handed piano or pocket billiards.

When asked what he would want to say to students, Senator Inouye recalled a special conversation with his father: "On the day of my U.S. Army enlistment, my father accompanied me to the point of departure. He was unusually quiet. Then he suddenly put his arm around my shoulder, and with unexpected eloquence, he told me that 'This country has been good to us. We owe much to this country. And now—I would never have chosen it to be this way—it is you who must try to return the goodness of this country. If it is necessary, you must be ready to give your life for it.' As he bid me farewell, my father said, 'Whatever you do, do not bring dishonor on our name.' I shall never forget his words."

Maxine Hong Kingston

Maxine Hong Kingston, author and educator, remembers her first writing, a poem, when she was eight years old. Writing this poem was much more interesting to Maxine than finishing her assignment of drawing a California map. While acquiring a second language and a new culture during her childhood years, she thought about ideas for her poems in Chinese, but wrote in English. Young Maxine did not fully understand how she was able to write in this way, but was soon able to move from writing poetry to completing book-length stories. Ms. Kingston later reflected that by first learning Chinese and then English, she became very interested in the use of language and putting it into story form. Through her three books, *The Woman Warrior*, *China Men*, and *Tripmaster Monkey*, she has blended together Chinese folklore, Chinese-American history, and the Chinese language with American culture, literature, and language.

Maxine Hong Kingston was born in Stockton, California, on October 27, 1940, the eldest of six children. Maxine's father was a scholar and schoolteacher in his village of Sun Woi near Canton, China. He decided to leave for America in search of a better life, and there he gave himself the name of Tom, after Thomas Edison. He worked for fifteen years in a New York laundry before he was able to send for his wife, Ying Lan. During the years that her husband was in New York, Ying Lan studied medicine and midwifery. She returned to the village of Sun Woi to set up a medical practice. This was considered to be quite an accomplishment for a woman at that time.

When Tom Hong was able to send for his wife, they settled together in Stockton, where he had a job managing a gambling house. Their daughter, Maxine, was named after a blonde woman gambler who always had the good fortune of winning.

Tom and Ying Lan Hong later bought and operated Stockton's New Port Laundry, which provided work for the Hong family, including their three sons and three daughters. New Port Laundry became a gathering place for many of the Chinese who lived in the community. Here they exchanged stories with the Hongs about the variety of roads that led them to finally settle in Stockton. Several of these people came from different parts of China, bringing colorful tales of local history and folklore to their new home. As the Hongs' oldest child, Maxine listened to and remembered the many stories she heard

Maxine Hong Kingston after completing her book, Tripmaster
Monkey

Two stories that Maxine has recalled that were later
blended with her own writing are "The Adventures of
General Yu Fei" and "The Ballad of Mu Lan." The first
story is about a mother who teaches her son, Yu Fei, the
importance of loyalty by tattooing words on his back that
would remind him of this lesson. The second story was

sung to Maxine by her mother. Mu Lan's father was an aging member of the army. Mu Lan disguises herself as a man, trades places with her father, and eventually becomes a general in the army. These stories, in addition to movies about Chinese swordsmen, made a great impression on young Maxine and later became a part of one of her books, *The Woman Warrior.*

Maxine, or "Ting Ting" as she was called by her family, spoke Say Yup, a dialect of Cantonese, when she started school. Her parents did not speak English and did not provide English language instruction before she started school. When Ting Ting entered kindergarten and had to speak English for the first time, she became silent. Later, she has recalled that she enjoyed the silence and did not realize that she was supposed to talk or go on to first grade from kindergarten. During this time she was also learning about American customs. Ting Ting gained her classmates' attention by drinking water from a toy saucer after the water had overflowed out of the cup. They laughed and pointed at her. Thinking that she was gaining acceptance and approval from the other students, she did it over and over again. At the time, she did not know that Americans do not drink from saucers, they drink from cups. In the second grade, she had difficulty with another American custom of singing "My County 'Tis of Thee," especially with the line, ". . . land where my fathers died . . ." She could not explain to her teacher that in the Chinese culture, talking about her father dying would bring a curse to her family.

Ting Ting's imagination and creativity surfaced again

and again throughout her elementary school years. Her parents were called to school to conferences with the teacher about her paintings of houses, flowers, and suns that she covered over with layers of black paint, and the drawings on the blackboard that she covered with layers of chalk. Her parents, who did not speak English, could not offer the concerned teacher any explanation. However, little Ting Ting knew that the black coverings she made were really stage curtains ready to open on fantastic plays and operas. This practice resulted in an IQ of zero on Ting Ting's first grade records when she colored the entire test page with black. Her mother and father, who did not approve of any disobedience in school and, hoping to impress this point upon their daughter, later reminded her that in China, parents and teachers of criminals were often executed.

In addition to her mother's stories, cultural beliefs instilled in Ting Ting Hong from childhood also reappear in her adult writings. In the Chinese culture, males are generally considered first, then girls. While helping at her parents' laundry, young Maxine would hear sayings like "Better to raise geese than girls," or stories about poor families that sold their daughters as slaves. Although her parents had no intention of selling her, little Ting Ting decided to take on the spirit of the woman warrior of her later book to fight any possibility of enslavement. She threw screaming and crying fits, walked with a limp, would not cook, and dropped food dishes on guests to make sure she would be undesirable as a slave.

After American school, Maxine and her younger sister

attended Chinese school from 5:00 to 7:00 P.M. At this school, the Chinese girls were not silent. They recited lessons orally to their teacher, and during recess they played "capture-the-flag," screaming and yelling and sometimes ended up in fistfights. As she entered the upper grades in her elementary school, Maxine became more vocal and her schoolwork began to improve. She has remembered the feeling of power that came with speaking, writing, and expressing herself in the English language. Throughout junior high and high school Maxine's writing included poems, ghost stories, fairy tales, and skits. Several of her teachers encouraged her writing, and at the age of fifteen she won a five-dollar award from *Girl Scout Magazine*. Her winning essay, about her experiences as a Chinese-American girl, was titled, "I Am an American."

In 1958, she enrolled at the University of California at Berkeley as an engineering major. Although excellent in math, Maxine decided to switch her major to English during her second year. She did well in school and was awarded a series of eleven scholarships that helped her to finish college. While attending Berkeley, she met Earll Kingston, who appeared with her in *Galileo*, a student-produced play. They married in 1962 after Maxine graduated. Together, Maxine and Earll marched in protest against the Vietnam War, became ordained ministers of the Universal Life Church, and later taught at a ghetto school in Hayward, just south of Berkeley. Their son, Joseph, was born in 1963, a year before Maxine went back to school for her teaching credentials.

During the late sixties, the Kingstons moved to Hawaii and Maxine began her first two books. Maxine took different teaching jobs at public and private schools, while Earll worked with a Shakespearean theater group. When Maxine was not teaching creative writing at school, she was writing herself. Her first two award-winning books, *The Woman Warrior* (1976) and *China Men* (1980) tell about Chinese women and Chinese men, how they came to the United States, and how they became a part of America. These books are written in a style of writing or storytelling, which in Hawaii is called "talk story," where personal experiences, history, myths, and legends are woven together. In 1976, *The Woman Warrior* was recognized as best nonfiction book by the National Book Critics Circle. *China Men* is noted for retelling the history of Chinese men who came to America to work in the Hawaiian sugarcane fields or to build the transcontinental railroad, their achievements, and the discrimination they faced in establishing a new home.

Her third book, *Tripmaster Monkey* (1989), is about a fictional character named Wittman Ah Sing, a fifth-generation Chinese-American Berkeley graduate living during the sixties. Wittman loses his job as a department store toy salesman and begins to write a play based on an old Chinese story. The main character reflects Maxine Hong Kingston's interest in the theater and acting, as well as her college background. This book, like the first two, blends facts and folk legends. *Tripmaster Monkey* uses American slang and more modern language, different from *The Woman Warrior* and *China Men*, where readers

Portrait photograph of Maxine Hong Kingston with one of her best-selling books

were given a feel for the rich, singsong rhythm of the Chinese language.

Maxine Hong Kingston believes that as a professional writer she has the ability to influence many people with her ideas. She has become a "Woman Warrior" herself, using the power of the pen rather than the sword. When she sits down to write, she lets her thoughts and feelings flow freely from her imagination and onto the paper. After she records her main story ideas, she will revise and rewrite her story several times until it reads smoothly and she is satisfied. Sometimes her stories will start with a doodle or with a simple picture that she has drawn. Next, she may add words to the pictures and will then expand upon this by describing the scenery or the setting. Often, she does not know if her day of writing will bring a new twist to the story or if the story will come to an end.

In addition to her books, Ms. Kingston has also written short stories, poems, and several articles that have been published in magazines and journals. For these many achievements, she has been recognized by different organizations. The most distinguished was in 1980, when she became the first Chinese American to be named as a "Living Treasure of Hawaii." This award is given by a Buddhist sect located in Honolulu, Hawaii, and is usually presented to persons over the age of eighty. In 1989, she was one of the first recipients to receive the newly created Governor's Award for the Arts from the California Arts Council. A documentary about Maxine Hong Kingston has been completed to be televised across the United States by the Public Broadcasting System (PBS). She has also been acknowledged by the famous and luxurious Raffles Hotel in Singapore by having a room named after her.

During the mid-1980s, the Kingstons, with their son, Joseph, who is a musician, moved back to Oakland, California. Ms. Kingston is back at the college she graduated from as a teacher in the English department. Her leisure time is spent reading, studying Zen Buddhism, sewing, or gardening. She is still involved with politics. She has participated in a protest march against the killings in China's Tiananmen Square and has financially supported various liberal causes.

Maxine Hong Kingston continues with her writing. She is working on another novel, which will update Wittman Ah Sing's life from *Tripmaster Monkey* to present times. Her completed books remain popular and are read throughout the world in different language translations, including Chinese, Japanese, French, Italian, Dutch, Hebrew, and Norwegian. Her books have given readers a better understanding of the contributions from the Chinese people in the early development of our country. Her "talk stories" have also presented a picture of how the Chinese and American cultures, histories, and folklore have been blended to create unique individuals. Maxine Hong Kingston has said that writers can have as much power through their written words as the military has with their bullets. Utilizing her words, Ms. Kingston will continue to write stories that communicate her values and ideas toward accomplishing world peace.

June
Kuramoto

 "When I was very young, my mother took me to see Madame Kazue Kudo performing in a koto concert. I instantly fell in love with the harplike sound of this beautiful Japanese musical instrument. I begged my mother to ask Madame Kudo to teach me how to play the koto. My mother was shocked that this little kid would be asking to play such an instrument. Madame Kudo became my teacher and ever since then I have been studying the koto with her. Through the years, the koto has become a link between my two countries: Japan and America."

The musical group Hiroshima has woven together the instruments and music of Japan and America to create a unique jazz and rock style. The principal members of the group presently include: Dan Kuramoto, leader and keyboards/woodwinds; June Kuramoto, koto player; Danny

Yamamoto, drums; Johnny Mori, percussionist and taiko drums (large Japanese festival drums); and vocalist Machun. They have recorded over six successful record albums. For over fifteen years Hiroshima has been together recording and performing throughout the United States, Japan, and the Philippines.

June Okida Kuramoto was born in Saitama-ken, Japan, about a two-hour drive north of Tokyo, on July 22, 1948. She came with her family to the United States at the age of five and was raised in Los Angeles, California, with an older brother, Tracy, and two younger sisters, Julia and Eimie. When June's family first came to the United States, her mother joined a social welfare organization called Sakura Kai. The group's primary purpose was to help immigrant families from Japan ease into the American way of life. It was at one of the Sakura Kai activities that June first heard Madame Kudo play the koto. Throughout her childhood, June studied traditional koto music from Madame Kudo, eventually earning a Masters Degree from the famed Michio Miyagi Koto School of Tokyo. She took lessons once a week after her regular school day was over, and practiced one half to two hours a day. Although learning to play the koto was time-consuming, June's interest and love for this instrument was strong.

"I remember in the third grade we celebrated Girl's Day, a Japanese holiday on March 3. The teacher asked if I would bring something from my heritage to share. I walked ten blocks to school carrying my koto, which is six feet three inches long, nine inches wide, with thir-

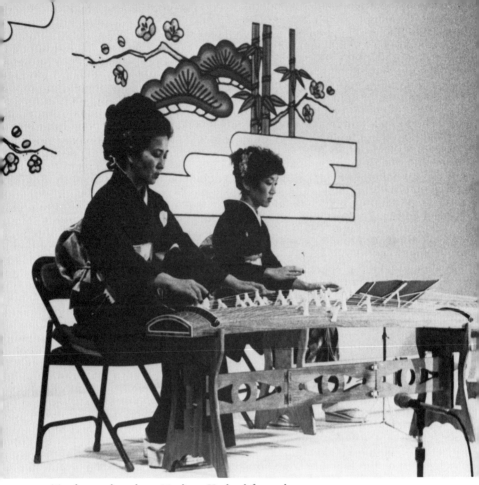

Teacher and student: Madame Kudo, left, and
June Kuramoto

teen strings, and small wooden bridges under the strings.
It weighs about fifteen to twenty pounds. I played a song
I was learning at a special assembly. I don't remember if
I tuned it correctly. I just remember how happy and
proud I was to play the koto."

In junior high school, June sometimes had difficulty
choosing between koto lessons and being with her friends.

"It's a tough age," June recalls. "Kids are very critical—you have to be 'in' and I wanted so much to belong. Some of the kids called the koto a 'grandma instrument' or 'grandma music' and they would make fun of me." June still loved to play the koto, but at one point it became necessary for Madame Kudo to pick June up from school to make sure she took her lessons. Peer pressure almost convinced June to stop. In high school, she did stop studying the koto for about one year. She began again after she realized how much she had missed it and how much it had meant to her—the discipline, the feeling of accomplishment after working hard to memorize a song, or as an outlet to express her thoughts and emotions. "I grumbled as a child with all the housework, and practicing I had to do. We were a poor family and nothing came easy. Now, when I look back, I am grateful because hard work made me stronger and a more responsible person."

Between high school and college, June developed a new form to her music. After beginning her koto studies again, she realized what had made her quit. Her teacher taught classical and traditional Japanese koto music. June felt that as a Japanese American, this style of koto music was not relevant to her experiences in America. She thought about more contemporary ways to bring Japanese and Western instruments together to express the two cultural backgrounds. The most natural accompaniment for the koto is the *shakuhachi*, or Japanese bamboo flute.

"I thought what about a Western flute? I asked Dan Kuramoto, the leader of Hiroshima if he would like to try blending the koto with the flute. I was a classically trained person and I only knew reading written music, and he was from a more jazz background with the ability to improvise. We exchanged learning techniques, but it was a struggle for me to improvise. He taught me to listen to my heart where the music comes from and to hear my own songs." Dan and June married in 1971 and have one daughter, Lani. Although now divorced, they continue their working relationship with their music and in the raising of their daughter.

Eventually, other instruments were added to the flute and koto, including keyboards, woodwinds, drums, bass, and guitar. June's koto added a new dimension to the group's music, creating a distinct sound and style that was Japanese-American. Although June was criticized by some people, who thought that combining classical koto music with Western instruments was "vulgar," the majority of the Asian community strongly supported and identified with this new form of music. The group's music was further expanded by adding percussion and the Japanese taiko drums.

Hiroshima has recorded albums for Arista Records and Epic-CBS/Sony Records. Their albums are titled *Hiroshima* (1979), *Odori* (1981), *Third Generation* (1983), *Another Place* (1985), *Go* (1987), and *East* (1989). *"Odori"* is the Japanese word for "dance"; *"go"* is the number five in Japanese, and this was the group's fifth album.

The name of the group, Hiroshima, reflects pride in their Asian-American heritage and serves as a reminder in support of world peace. Their music has earned im-

*Members of Hiroshima. Left to right: June Kuramoto, koto;
Danny Yamamoto, drums; Dan Kuramoto, keyboards, woodwinds;
Johnny Mori, taiko, percussion; Machun, vocals, guitar.*

pressive awards, such as *Performance* magazine's Breakout
Artist of the Year (1980), Grammy nomination (1981),
Best Live Jazz Group from *Cashbox* (1987), and Best Jazz
Album, *Go*, from Soul Train Music Awards (1988). The
album *Go* held the number one spot for eight weeks on
the *Billboard* Contemporary Jazz Album chart.

During the 1980s, Ms. Kuramoto fulfilled her desire
to write songs. Reading Western music was unfamiliar
to June, since koto music is written in Japanese characters
instead of musical notes. In addition, each Japanese instrument has its own music. She was able to read koto
music, but the *shakuhachi* (bamboo flute) used a completely different set of characters for its music. She studied

music theory and composition with Mocair Santos, a noted Brazilian composer and arranger. Mocair Santos taught June rhythms and how to read Western music. "He is an excellent teacher, especially when teaching children. He made me hum the rhythms. I started humming rhythms on my own and those developed into melodies for me."

Writing music has become an absorbing interest for Ms. Kuramoto. The ideas for her songs come from images that surround her daily life or from what she has experienced. She began working with a collaborator, Derek Nakamoto, who extended her ideas and original melodies. She now collaborates with other writers. The first song that she wrote is called "Distant Thoughts." June explained that the idea for "Distant Thoughts" came from her fascination with UFOs, the movie character E.T., and a friend's song on the same subject titled "Distant Stranger."

One of her more recent songs was inspired by a book, *Sadako and a Thousand Paper Cranes*, that June's daughter, Lani, shared with her. In 1945, the first atomic bomb exploded over Hiroshima, Japan. The story's main character, Sadako Sasaki, was two years old when she was exposed to the atomic radiation which eventually caused her death from leukemia ten years later. In the last months of her terrible illness, Sadako followed the Japanese tradition of folding a thousand paper cranes, which is believed to bring good health and long life. In the Hiroshima Peace Park in Japan, there is a statue of Sadako holding a golden crane in her hands, built from funds raised by Sadako's family, friends, and other schoolchildren. Today, people worldwide send paper cranes to decorate Sadako's statue and to give the message of world peace. A year after reading the book, Lani's grandmother was diagnosed with cancer. Lani wanted to make a thousand cranes for her Grandma. Everywhere June and Lani went, they folded paper cranes in their spare moments. "We folded cranes on airplanes, in restaurants, at band rehearsals. People asked us what we were doing and after we told them, they wanted to learn how to make the cranes, too. We would show them how and they would give us the cranes they made." After two years June and her daughter finished the thousand cranes. They feel fortunate that Lani's grandmother is still living and enjoying her special gift.

When June told a friend about this experience, he suggested making a thousand cranes to help heal Mother Earth that has become diseased with careless pollution. June's friend thought an even better idea would be for June to write a song called "Thousand Cranes."

"I thought about Sadako and felt the emotion of her experience and what Mother Earth must be feeling, too. Sometimes when the experience is so powerful, the song just comes out. I sent my song 'Thousand Cranes' to Derek and he added a chorus. I decided that it should have vocals just on the chorus and wrote the lyrics. 'Thousand Cranes' was quick. It just came to us. We didn't have to slowly pound it out or think about it for a long time."

June Kuramoto and daughter, Lani, wearing Japanese kimonos

Another part of World War II history, the imprisonment of families of Japanese ancestry living on the West Coast, has given June another idea to consider for a song. Between 1942 and 1945 over 110,000 persons of Japanese ancestry were held in internment camps surrounded by barbed-wire fences and patrolled by armed military guards. These persons were believed to be a threat to U.S. national security. Men, women, and children, the majority being American citizens, were forced to stay in one of ten relocation camps in remote areas of the United States. However, Japanese living in Hawaii and east of California, Oregon, and Washington were not put into relocation camps.

"I feel angry and hurt for what my father's family had to endure. There are bitter feelings from older relatives because they feel some of the best years were taken. Some had successful businesses or owned property and after the war much was lost. I see now how difficult it must have been. They were torn between not wanting to put up with the situation and needing to protect the welfare of their families. Nobuko Miyamoto wrote a song called 'Gaman' (which means 'to endure' in Japanese) about this experience and I played koto on it. I realize now that I have my own feelings about this time and I need to be a voice for the Issei and Nisei (first- and second-generation Japanese)."

In 1989, a world premiere production of the play, *Sansei*, was presented by the Los Angeles County Music Center and Center Theatre Group. The play offered experiences of Hiroshima's core band members (Dan Kuramoto, June, Yamamoto, and Mori) growing up in Los

*Playing
the koto during
the play,* Sansei

Angeles as "Sansei," third-generation Japanese Americans. The idea for *Sansei* originated from an earlier play about the Hispanic culture called *Zoot Suit*. Dan Kuramoto collaborated with Daniel Valdez to compose and arrange the music for *Zoot Suit*, directed by Luis Valdez. Like *Zoot Suit*, *Sansei* presents a personal portrait of one culture through drama and music. At each performance of *Sansei*, the audience was asked to fold a paper crane in memory of Sadako and to promote international peace and understanding. At the close of the play, the cranes were given to a representative of the city of Hiroshima to be placed on Sadako's monument in Japan.

In addition to recording with Hiroshima, June Kuramoto has performed with other musicians in concerts and recordings, and has worked on musical scoring for movies and television. Some of these musicians include Ravi Shankar, Taste of Honey, Manhattan Transfer, Stanley Clarke, Brothers Johnson, Makoto, Lou Gramm of the group Foreigner, Nobuko Miyamoto, Angela Bofill, Kazu Matsui, Martika, and Teddy Pendergrass. Although June has expanded her koto music into jazz, rock, soul, and funk, she does not think of herself as a great koto player or songwriter.

"I see myself as a human being first, then a musician. I present a different picture of Asian Americans than the stereotyped images that have been portrayed in the media.

"Before I started writing songs I needed to develop more confidence in myself. I feel everyone has a song inside. It's a matter of whether it can be brought out. I take a risk every time someone else listens to a new song that I have written. I need to take chances and reach out of my dreams or they may never come true."

June Okida Kuramoto would like to be remembered as a musician and as a person who worked hard and as honestly as possible for what she believed in—someone who "did not give up, kept a positive attitude, and made things happen."

Haing Ngor

"In 1977, I saw a young lady, seventeen years old at most, and she had infections in her eyes. She could not open them; she had pus. She was in bad condition, and I felt it was very hard to make a decision. If I treated that young lady, maybe I would be killed by the Khmer Rouge. I was a doctor. I saw before my eyes patients, sick people, mothers and children, but how could I help them? They died on the path going to work, those children, yelling, 'Please, please give me a spoon of rice.' But how could I get rice for them? Even for myself, I had no rice. For everybody, there was no food.

"She cried the whole time, 'Please help me, my eyes cannot open.' Finally, I asked permission from the Khmer Rouge chief to bring her to a hospital. He wrote on a piece of paper—not good paper but from a cigarette—

and let me go. I thought that at least I was doing something for her. So I brought her there. How old was the Khmer surgeon? At most, he was twelve years old. He just got up from the garden, wiped his hands, and went to what was not really an operating room. I waited and saw. He got needles and said, 'I will treat you, no problem, and after two or three days you can go back to work.' He opened up the lady's eyes and he used needles and screwed into her eyes. Then, after that, she had terrible pain. Three days later, both her eyes were blind. I was very upset. Why had I brought that young lady to a hospital? Now who would be responsible for her life?"

Dr. Haing Ngor survived starvation, torture, the deaths of his wife and parents, and bloody war in Cambodia. For over ten years, he has asked himself why he was spared. "Maybe God saved my life to let me be an ambassador, to tell the world what happened in my country, to help the children at the border refugee camps." At first, that was difficult, he says, and nobody seemed to listen. He says people were usually more interested in Vietnam. "In 1979, I got out from Cambodia. I got into a camp. I talked to the refugees. I told television, newspapers—nothing. After the movie, it was 'Yes, Cambodia.' "

That movie was *The Killing Fields*, released in 1984. The film made more people aware of the tragedy in Cambodia, also known as Kampuchea. In a strange irony, Dr. Ngor portrayed Dith Pran, another Cambodian who had survived similar horrors. Dr. Ngor had never wanted to be an actor, but that performance won him an Oscar.

Haing Ngor in the movie The Killing Fields

More importantly, his new fame offered him the chance to be heard and to help.

Haing Ngor grew up in the quiet village of Samrong Yong. Phnom Penh, the capital of Cambodia, was to the north. Even as a young boy, Haing knew firsthand that there was political unrest in his country. France had controlled Cambodia for nearly one hundred years, but guerrillas were rebelling. Haing's family was caught in the middle. His parents were kidnapped, his father several times by both sides. Each time a ransom was paid for his release. Haing's father was a merchant who had a store, then a lumber mill and a fuel business. The family had eight children, five boys and three girls. Ngor, the family name, traditionally comes first, and so his name was really Ngor Haing, but he is better known today as Haing Ngor.

Haing Ngor admits that he first wanted to become a doctor to earn plenty of money, but he also had other reasons. "There were many sick people in Cambodia. My village was very far from the capital. Hygiene was not good and families had a very bad health situation. I wanted to be clean and help the people. I saw children, old people, wounded people, many in rural villages, but no medicine. As a doctor, at least I could do something for my village."

Haing Ngor attended medical school in Phnom Penh, and his classes were in French. While in school, Haing needed money and worked part-time as a tutor. A girl named Chang My Huoy became one of his pupils, and over a year later, his girl friend. Their courtship was very proper under the supervision of Chang My Huoy's mother.

Since there were not enough doctors in Cambodia, the medical students were permitted to practice before they had actually graduated. Haing worked in both a military hospital and a private clinic. He chose to specialize in obstetrics and gynecology, treating women and delivering babies. At the same time, he operated the family gasoline business and prospered. Huoy liked her position as a teacher. He recalls, "In 1968, I got two Mercedes. I paid cash. One was for my girl friend. I let her have her own car and I had mine. I would say, 'Don't cook. We will go out to eat.' " Dr. Ngor finally received his medical degree in February, 1975. He led a privileged life, worked in his clinic, and enjoyed a respect he thought would last throughout his career.

Even though there were already seeds of trouble, Cambodia seemed relatively quiet to Haing Ngor until 1970. Prince Sihanouk, the country's leader, was deposed in a coup, and General Lon Nol became head of the new government. War still raged in Vietnam, affecting Cambodia. Also during the early 1970s, a Cambodian Communist group known as the Khmer Rouge gained strength and territory as they opposed Lon Nol. They overtook the village of Samrong Yong in 1972 and Haing Ngor's parents moved to Phnom Penh, but the Ngors did not want to leave their country. By 1975, the Khmer Rouge approached the capital, but Dr. Ngor was enjoying his position and still believed there would be a peaceful settlement. He did not think his city would fall.

"April 17, 1975, and then 'Bang!' Just like that, everything was gone." Dr. Ngor was operating on a patient when some Khmer Rouge rebels entered his clinic. One put a gun to Haing Ngor's head and asked if he was the doctor. Very quickly, Dr. Ngor realized the danger. He replied that the doctor had left, and then he fled moments later with his staff. The unconscious patient with his body still cut open was left to die, but Dr. Ngor felt they all would have died if they had remained.

People were herded from the city into the countryside. They were forced to live and do physical work for the new regime in primitive conditions. There was not enough food, but anyone caught with a private garden or even picking wild plants was punished. Haing Ngor and Huoy both hid their status, fearing it could get them killed. Dr. Ngor would not wear his eyeglasses and insisted he was a taxi driver.

Dr. Ngor says that during those years, "There was no school, paper, pencils. The children were told their school was on the farm, to learn how to dig, how to plant rice." He says that often the Khmer Rouge who guarded him were children and they did not understand what real education was, why a person had to go to school to be a doctor, lawyer, or teacher. "One, at most sixteen years old, said, 'I am a doctor. Do you want me to take your stomach out? I can do it. Why do you have to go to learn for seven years to be a doctor?' Yes, he could take it out, but he could not put it back in."

Haing Ngor has reported that people were tortured as punishment or to force a confession, giving details of his own horrors. He was accused of stealing food, suspected of having military rank, and identified as a doctor. A portion of his little finger was chopped off. He was tied to a post with a fire lighted underneath and a plastic bag over his head, before he was spared. Another time, he was imprisoned in a filthy, infested hut which, after several days, was set afire. After each time, Huoy nursed him and tenderly cared for him.

Dr. Ngor tells how death was common, from torture and execution, from illness and starvation. It has been estimated that over one million people perished during this period of Cambodia's history. Haing Ngor's parents and many of his siblings did not survive. Huoy died in his arms on June 2, 1978. She was pregnant, but was malnourished and weak. When she went into labor prematurely and had trouble, Dr. Ngor even tried to get her to a hospital. "My wife's death was caused by many factors. She had depression. Secondly, she died of starvation, after three to four months with no food. Even I ate centipedes, snails, grasshoppers, mice, anything to survive. Then, the baby was premature. At the time, if I had had enough medical equipment, I think I could have saved her. But there were spies everywhere. If I made the decision to save her life, would she survive? There was no medicine, no sterility. Why couldn't I save her life? She saved my life. I still remember at the last minute she cried out, 'Sweetheart, give me a last kiss.' I still love her."

As the politics changed in Cambodia, Haing Ngor was able to escape to Thailand in 1979. He practiced medicine

Dr. Ngor with a young girl in the Thai camp, before he left for the United States

again, and began to help his people, treating Cambodian refugees. In 1980, he was permitted to leave for the United States, and departed on a charter flight packed with other refugees. In Los Angeles, a cousin helped him find a small apartment. Dr. Ngor did not have a medical license to work as a doctor in the United States, so he took a position with the Chinatown Service Center helping Vietnamese, Cambodian, and Laotian refugees find jobs. He spoke many languages, so he and his clients could usually find one they both knew. Dr. Ngor also worked extra hours providing security outside a warehouse, although he says that at the time he could not afford a jacket.

Dr. Ngor was still living and working in Los Angeles when he was spotted by someone casting a movie about Cambodia. The film would be based on a story of a *New York Times* correspondent, Sydney Schanberg, and his Cambodian assistant, Dith Pran. It would show how Dith Pran survived the Khmer Rouge. Although when the movie was cast, people did not realize how closely Haing Ngor's experiences paralleled Dith Pran's, they would later learn that he had suffered even more, losing his wife and unborn child, while Dith Pran had been reunited with his wife and children.

Dr. Ngor went back to Thailand to film *The Killing Fields*, and then returned to his job at the Chinatown Service Center, working quietly. The movie was critically acclaimed as soon as it was released in 1984. For his portrayal of Dith Pran, Haing Ngor won an Oscar in the category of best supporting actor in March, 1985. Once again, Dr. Ngor tasted a glamorous life. However, he could not and did not want to forget his Cambodian experiences. He had not wanted to be an actor, but realized there would be rewards. He left the Service Center and channeled his fame, and the money it brought, toward telling the world about Cambodia and helping its refugees. On television, he appeared on "Miami Vice," "China Beach," in a *National Geographic* program, and in other productions. He had other movie roles. He told his own story in almost five hundred horrifying yet spellbinding pages in his autobiography, *A Cambodian Odyssey*, written with Roger Warner. Some chapters of that book are so gory that they begin by warning the reader. Another book, *The Healing Fields*, will concern refugees all over the world. Dr. Ngor still lives in the same simple apartment. He drove the same Volkswagen for nine years, and after that one, he vowed to buy another.

Dr. Ngor works continuously for peace in Cambodia and on behalf of refugees, especially children. He raises money, and most of what he has earned from his acting roles, book royalties, and lecturing has gone toward relief organizations and medical care. He often travels to refugee camps to treat patients, and he wants to build a hospital. He and Dith Pran, now a photographer for *The New York Times*, are good friends and both are visible spokesmen. Dr. Ngor says, "We have the same goals. On the East Coast, Dith Pran, on the West Coast, Dr. Haing Ngor. Sometimes when Dith Pran flies to the West Coast, I say laughing, 'You violate my territory!' "

In August, 1989, both men returned to Cambodia for the first time since they fled. Dr. Ngor was tearfully reunited with a surviving brother who was very poor. "I thought he would ask for money, but instead he asked, 'Could you give that shirt to me?' " Dr. Ngor took off

Dr. Haing Ngor signing autographs after a fund-raising event

his shirt, and then gladly provided him with other shirts, pants, a jacket, and coat. Another brother, Dr. Ngor's youngest, lives near Los Angeles and owns a donut shop.

When Dr. Ngor first came to the United States, he took classes, intending to get an American medical license. However, he did not complete the requirements before *The Killing Fields* brought instant fame. He would still like to get that license "one day," then adds, "but now is the right time to help people first. One day I will go back to medical school. Whether I pass the exam or not, I will just go to school to learn more."

Haing Ngor did not postpone becoming an American citizen. He valued the freedom it symbolized and offered. He beams, "I am very proud to have an adopted mother, the U.S.A." He also understood the advantages of a United States passport for visiting other countries. "I got citizenship and it is easy to go help and tell the world to help my people."

Dr. Ngor thinks children are very special. "I want to see that the children go back to school in my country. Education is a helpful means to develop and build and heal the nation. Like a house, the children are the columns of the nation. If the columns are strong, the house is strong." He wipes his eyes when pointing out that over half of more than 300,000 refugees in Thailand are children, many of them orphans. He would like to sponsor some to come to the United States, and wants to adopt several himself. He wonders if American children realize how lucky they are, and says poetically, "Children at the border—who helps them, who embraces them? Just the wind. No one comes to help them. What kind of blanket do they have? Just their skin. What kind of food do they have? Just the water. What kind of house? The sky and the jungle. It is completely different."

Dustin Nguyen

 The television program "21 Jump Street" was usually about four young undercover police officers posing as high school students, gang members, or drug dealers, so that they could better fight crime in their city. The action often took place with car chases, fistfights, or classroom antics. Yet one special episode of this TV series was very different. It was set during a bloody war, had an unusual amount of violence, and took place thousands of miles from the familiar setting. The fall of Saigon, the capital of South Vietnam, was the unlikely subject of that episode, but it had been a very real and brutal experience for cast member Dustin Nguyen. The event was recreated to explain the background of his character, Harry Ioki, a Vietnamese American who had taken a Japanese name. The segment was also similar to Dustin's own escape, and even showed the gunning down of his best friend as they fled toward a ship near the beach.

Dustin Nguyen was successful in his role as Harry Ioki. He earned enough to buy a four-bedroom house in Costa Mesa, near Los Angeles. He has raced as a celebrity entrant in the Toyota Grand Prix in Long Beach. He enjoys his motorcycle and skiing. Once again he lives a secure life, after his comfortable childhood was suddenly thrown into turmoil, and his family had to start all over in a different country with a foreign language, poorer jobs, and no home. Dustin worked his way back up, but he does not forget what it was like to be a refugee or a teenager or Vietnamese. His role in "21 Jump Street" spoke against drugs, gangs, and prejudice, and Dustin does the same in his private life.

Dustin Nguyen was born Nguyen Xuan Tri on September 17, 1962. He lived in a custom-built house with his parents and younger brother. A maid took care of the beautiful home which had been designed by his father, who was a television producer, actor, and director. His mother was an actress and dancer. The family lived very well in Saigon. Vietnam had been a French colony from the mid-1880s until the 1940s, so for many years there was French influence on Vietnamese society, including education. Dustin vividly remembers that the schools were very competitive and strict.

"From ages one to five, I went to a French kindergarten, so I spoke French probably better than I spoke Vietnamese at that time. After that, my parents enrolled me in a public school system. There was an entrance exam

A casual shot of Dustin Nguyen

to enter each new phase. After sixth grade, there was a two-day exam to get into a prestigious high school. Out of five thousand students, only five hundred qualified. I enjoyed school and being in the top 5 percent. They used to announce the top student each month." He tells how that person was respected and "would get elected to do certain duties. There was a marching group, and I was very proud to be chosen to lead.

"We had to wear uniforms, a white shirt and navy blue pants, and there was discipline." Even with this atmosphere, Dustin says that many students rebelled, although he recounts a real fear of the teachers because punishment "was 'whack' with a ruler." He says that many children behaved rigidly when in school, but "outside had a totally different personality."

Dustin's student days, and his whole life, changed when he was twelve. His father had written propaganda programs which urged the North Vietnamese to defect and join the South Vietnamese in the ongoing war. When the North Vietnamese entered Saigon in April of 1975, the Nguyen family knew they would have to escape. If Mr. Nguyen were caught by the North Vietnamese, his crime against them could have been punished by death. There was no time or way to take much from their home. The few items they did take on the boat were either stolen or lost. The escape itself was harrowing, as Dustin's family was separated. He and his best friend tried to run toward a rescue ship as the North Vietnamese soldiers known as the Viet Cong fired their rifles at those who fled. As Dustin watched in horror, his friend was shot and instantly killed. Dustin had to continue and swam toward

Dustin at about age eleven with his mother

the boat. Once on board, he found his parents and brother, and their new life began.

First, they stopped for three weeks on the island of Guam, a U.S. territory in the Pacific Ocean. From there, the family went to Fort Chaffee, Arkansas, where there was a camp for the refugees. The American government had established several camps to help refugees adapt to life in the United States. One big adjustment would be language. Dustin knew Vietnamese and French, but no English. His parents urged him to learn from teachers at the camp. Dustin's mother spent much of the time hospitalized. She had been pregnant but miscarried. His father worked to find a sponsor who would get the family out of the camp and into American society.

The Nguyens were of the Buddhist religion, like many Vietnamese, but the Methodist Church generously sponsored them. The family was sent to live with a woman in her home of Kirkwood, Missouri, near St. Louis. Other people helped the family get donated clothing and jobs. In Vietnam, Dustin's parents had had creative positions, but in America his father started as a dishwasher and janitor, while his mother began as a cleaning lady. The family was very grateful, though. With hard work and more help, they received a bank loan and were able to buy a house of their own once again, though much smaller than the one they had left behind in Saigon.

The family was also given more English lessons, and Dustin even used "Sesame Street" on TV to help him learn the language. The Nguyens were the first Vietnamese in the area, and Dustin had some trouble in his new school. He was put in the eighth grade, but says he was teased and found it difficult to make friends. He was a shy person and did not feel confident speaking English, but it was something he realized he had to do. "Even at that age, I understood that this was where I was going to spend the rest of my life, and I made a real effort to learn the language. If I were to give advice, that would be 'number one,' " he says, speaking directly to those who have had a similar experience. "When you come over to a country and are surrounded by your people in a community, you tend not to have to learn the language as much as if you are isolated. English is the one thing that makes it a lot easier, because from there a lot of your other problems resolve themselves. The ability to communicate is so important at that age. You want to be able to have friends, and to be accepted. You must have a desire to learn it, rather than thinking 'English lessons today, ugh!' "

He offers another tip. "I love to read. Reading will improve language skills and just general education. One of the books that influenced me is *Jonathan Livingston Seagull* by Richard Bach. It is a really simple book to read and is about a seagull who refuses to be just a seagull. It is a good book to motivate you to achieve things in life, rather than just continue an everyday routine."

Language was not the only adjustment Dustin confronted. He says that for young Asian Americans, as well as children of other cultures, "having to adapt, learning a new language, and being able to retain your heritage is very confusing. Often, parents are not as eager to make the transition, and rightfully so. Some of the traditional values offer a different perspective of the American way. In addition, there is the generation gap." He says that even while learning English, it is important to remember that a sense of heritage must be kept. "This can be difficult to do. There is a line, 'Are you becoming Americanized?' That is not an accurate word. You have to keep a sense of both." He says that to deny heritage "probably stems from peer pressure and the feeling of having to blend into the society and say, 'I am not black, I am not Hispanic, or I am not Vietnamese. I am just like you.' "

He thinks children should resist the temptation to want to be like everyone else.

Dustin was progressing in Kirkwood, but at times he

Dustin Nguyen, center, at his Kirkwood High School graduation

still felt alone and unhappy. Then, at fourteen, he began to study martial arts. He especially enjoyed Tae Kwon Do and earned his second degree black belt when he was seventeen. He also became a Midwestern champion, and even taught the skills. "Martial arts became a very big part of my life, with the discipline and physical and spiritual side. I was not good at any other sports, and that had been difficult. To be able to compete was prestigious and provided me with a sense of self-confidence and accomplishment. From there, I knew that I could be successful in other things in life."

After graduating from Kirkwood High School, Dustin entered Orange Coast College in California. Though they were successful, Dustin's parents had never graduated from college. They badly wanted their sons to earn college degrees. They wanted Dustin to be an engineer, but he was drawn to acting. "I was not really planning on becoming an actor, but I enrolled in an acting class because I was really shy. My friends encouraged me. Once I started studying acting, I was fascinated by it and discovered that it was really healthy for me. Then came the transition of plunging forward, becoming an actor, and making a living at it."

Dustin's parents did not approve of his decision to become an actor. "There were a few disagreements on my decision to drop out of school, but I wanted to do it so badly and I knew I could be successful. A sacrifice was being apart from my family, both physically and emotionally, a terrible thing to go through." Dustin and his parents have since reconciled. He says, "Now they are proud and very supportive."

Dustin was also ready to endure other hardships. "I had to be willing to lose everything. Acting is such an insecure and illogical profession." He says that people studying to be engineers or doctors go through steps and are almost guaranteed employment, but actors are not. He emphasizes that it is difficult to earn a good salary while trying to become an actor because at any time there must be a willingness to interrupt a job for an audition.

By the time Dustin Nguyen moved to Hollywood, he had legally changed his name and become an American

Dustin Nguyen signing autographs at Camp Fire's Teens in Action program to promote awareness and prevention of teen suicide

citizen. During his first year, he studied acting, and auditioned, but without much luck. Rejection was hard, yet he was persistent. After trying out for an episode of "Magnum, P.I.," he was so nervous that he stayed with friends rather than be alone in his own apartment. He got the part. After that, he appeared in "General Hospital" for seven months.

From 1986 through 1990, he played the role of Harry Ioki in "21 Jump Street," filmed in Vancouver, British Columbia, Canada. He spoke about his daily life when he was working on the series. "As an actor in a television series, I work five days a week, with very irregular hours. For me, one episode, one hour, is a product of seven to eight working days, averaging fourteen hours a day. If daylight is required, we start early. If the sunrise is at five, we start about four to allow time for makeup, wardrobe, and equipment set-up. If nighttime is needed, we do not go to work until late afternoon, and we work until the next morning.

"I get my scripts several days before starting that particular episode. While doing one show, I am thinking about the next because I have the script in my hand. I am juggling. I get familiar with the script, but there is not much rehearsal with a television series. As they are setting up the equipment, which takes time, I get together with the actors and director and rehearse on the set. We do a blocking, which means staging the actual movement of the scene, and then start filming. Sometimes we do about four or five takes, but we are competing against time to finish in seven days."

As policeman Harry Ioki fought to make the streets safer, Dustin Nguyen persists, but more peaceably, against drugs and gangs. "I have always lent a hand to DARE (Drug Abuse Resistance Education) which is now a national program in America." DARE involves schools and police departments, and it begins in elementary school. In a series of classes and talks, children are taught why they should not take drugs and how to say "No" to them. "I go with officers to different schools, they have a big assembly, and we talk about drugs, educating the students. The DARE program goes beyond 'Just Say No,' to analyze why kids take drugs, the peer pressure and self-confidence elements." He says that there can be efforts against one side, the drug dealers, but drugs are sold because there is a demand, so the demand side should be eliminated. He emphasizes that if people do not take drugs, the dealers will have no buyers.

Gangs are another concern for Dustin, "particularly Asian-American, Vietnamese gangs." He says that sometimes both parents are working hard to support the family, but the children, lacking supervision, become wild. "No role model or authority figure, or just someone they respect, is guiding, so they join gangs as a substitution for family atmosphere. From then on, other things happen." Dustin feels very strongly about discouraging gang involvement, and is pleased that he can help. "That is the wonderful part, besides just entertaining people, to be able to affect the kids."

Dustin Nguyen is intent on improving as an actor. He also wants a bigger role in Hollywood itself, to choose projects, produce, and perhaps to direct. He relishes the opportunity to represent the Vietnamese favorably and to inspire children, especially those who are Asian. "When I was growing up, I was desperately searching for that role model. There are a lot of problems trying to adapt to a new culture. If I can exert a certain amount of positive influence, then I am very happy with that."

Ellison S. Onizuka

". . . Lt. Col. Ellison Onizuka had his life cut short for many reasons he could not control. Yet during his years, he accomplished much more than most. Our world is a better place for his being here. He will always be remembered."

—Neil A. Armstrong

 When Kichihei and Wakano Onizuka voyaged to Hawaii from the Fukuoka prefecture in Japan, they never dreamed that one day their grandson would fly among the stars. Kichihei and Wakano Onizuka first settled on the island of Oahu and began the backbreaking work of field hands on a large sugar plantation. Later they moved to the island of Hawaii and became farmers of the rich, desirable coffee beans of Kona. They raised their family of seven children

in the Japanese tradition and when their son, Masamitsu, became of age to be married, they called upon a *baishakunin*, or matchmaker, to find a wife for him. Mitsue Nagata, daughter of Kona coffee farmers, was chosen as Masamitsu's wife. Both Masamitsu and Mitsue were Nisei, or second-generation Japanese in America. They married and eventually opened a general merchandise store which supplied farmers with their daily needs in the village of Keopu, in northern Kona.

Ellison Onizuka was born on June 24, 1946, in the village of Keopu. He was the third of four children and the first son born to Masamitsu and Mitsue Onizuka. The two older children, Shirley and Norma, helped their parents by working in their store and taking care of their younger brothers, Ellison and Claude. Shirley remembers both boys as being very energetic in their childhood, especially Ellison, who also enjoyed satisfying his curiosity by taking apart watches or household objects to discover how things worked.

No one is sure when young Ellison first spoke about his dream of becoming an astronaut and traveling to the stars. Shirley has recalled one of Ellison's first experiences with rockets. One New Year's Eve, the family was inside the house when suddenly the floor began to vibrate and loud thumping noises were heard. Running outside, they could hear small explosions and could see smoke coming up from underneath the house. They soon discovered Ellison had set off a roman candle because he was interested to see how it worked!

Ellison's family encouraged him to apply his energy

and curiosity in school and extracurricular activities. He became a hardworking student who earned good grades and excelled in the areas of math and science. Ellison played team sports, participated in the Scouts, 4-H Club, and the Young Buddhist Association, and was elected to school and club leadership positions. He played basketball, but was better known as a center fielder on the 1962 and 1964 Big Island North Division championship baseball teams. As an Explorer Scout, he was recognized for his citizenship and commitment to community service, eventually achieving the honorable rank of Eagle Scout. Ellison is also remembered as a skilled "chicken dresser" by fellow 4-H members. He was among the best who entered the statewide contest to see how fast a chicken could be plucked and dressed.

In addition to his schooling and outside activities, Ellison had daily chores to do. Since he was the older brother, he was given more jobs than Claude. Ellison mostly helped in the family merchandise store, and during the late summer and fall would pick coffee beans in the family's fields. Kona schools were the only Hawaiian schools to take their summer vacation between August and November so that older children could help in the coffee fields. Ellison also worked part-time for Aloha Airlines and for a trucking company where he made deliveries to farms and stores in the Kona area.

In 1964, Ellison graduated from Konawaena High School with honors, and decided upon a career as an aerospace engineer. His mother, Mitsue Onizuka, has recalled the time when Ellison told his elementary school principal that he wanted to be an engineer. The principal visited the Onizuka home to find out the kind of engineering that interested him. His mother did not know, his sister thought he meant a train engineer, and Ellison said any kind would do as long as he could put "engineer" at the end of his name! It was not until high school that he decided upon aerospace engineering and applied to college at the Air Force Academy.

Although Ellison was not accepted by the Air Force Academy, his first choice, he felt enthusiastic about en-

Ellison Onizuka,
Eagle Scout, 1964

rolling at the University of Colorado. A 4-H educational scholarship from Standard Oil Company of three hundred dollars helped to get him started with college books and supplies. His mother and father approved of his decision to go on to college. As Ellison was growing up, his parents had little spare time to devote to his or any of their children's studies. However, through their years of hard work and savings, they were finally able to give him the valuable gift of a college education on the United States mainland. At the age of eighteen, Ellison left the friendliness of the warm, tropical Kona coast for the unfamiliarity of the cool, mountain, college town of Boulder, Colorado—his first long trip away from home into the unknown.

Ellison credited much of his adjustment to new independence to the confidence and discipline that he experienced in the Scouts. He devoted himself to his engineering studies and joined the university's Air Force ROTC program, where he was honored for his outstanding achievements. He also became involved in other college organizations and soon became recognized as a leader. Although his schooling was very important to him, Ellison also took time to socialize and relax. Winter vacations were often spent mastering the new sport of snow skiing, which was not quite as easy as riding sand-sliding boards on the beaches of Kona. Summers were spent at home with his family and friends in Keopu.

During Ellison's senior year at the University of Colorado, two memorable events occurred. Through his college roommate's girl friend, Ellison met Lorna Leiko

Yoshida. Like Ellison, Lorna was from a small community, Naalehu, on the island of Hawaii; active with the Young Buddhist Association; and participated in social clubs and organizations. She was attending Colorado State College, now known as the University of Northern Colorado. At first, Lorna recalled, she had an "egghead" picture of Ellison and thought he would be a "social nerd." She soon learned that in addition to his studious side, he also had a good sense of humor and was fun-loving. As third-generation Japanese in America—Sansei—they were able to choose their own spouses and did not have a *baishakunin* or go-between as required of their parents. They were married the day after Ellison's graduation in June at the Tri-State Buddhist Church in Denver. Only Ellison's mother was able to attend the wedding and graduation ceremonies. Just prior to these events, Masamitsu had suffered a fatal heart attack. This was a difficult time for Ellison, who had been very close to his father. In the Japanese tradition, family responsibility then falls upon the oldest son. When Ellison approached his mother with his plan to return home and help carry on the family business, she strongly told him to finish his schooling and fulfill his career as an aerospace engineer. She reminded Ellison that this is what his father would have wanted and that he had worked hard to give his oldest son the opportunity to make something of himself.

Ellison returned to his education and career with renewed energy and commitment to succeed. He graduated from the University of Colorado ROTC program as a second lieutenant, earned his Master of Science degree in aerospace engineering by December of 1969, and joined the United States Air Force in January, 1970. While in Colorado, his first child, Janelle, was born. After college, his home for the next four years was at McClellan Air Force Base in Sacramento, California, where he researched and designed flight test programs and aircraft safety systems. Ellison was next accepted to the Air Force Test Pilot School at Edwards Air Force Base in California's Mojave Desert, where he received flying instruction and completed courses in how to test new aircraft system designs. As an aerospace engineer, his job was to go with the test pilot on the new aircraft to determine if the different aircraft systems or machinery were properly designed and working while in flight. During his stay at Edwards Air Force Base, Darien, his second daughter, was born.

While Ellison Onizuka was testing aircraft and teaching test pilot school classes in engineering, NASA contacted civilian and military aeronautic organizations to recruit new astronauts. After the Apollo moon missions, the next big project became Skylab, an orbiting space station. In order to build Skylab, a "space shuttle" would be necessary to ferry specialists and materials back and forth. This shuttle would also need to be reusable, in order to keep the cost of each mission as low as possible. Eventually, a shuttle orbiter was built, which would be able to fly over a hundred space missions. The shuttle has three engines which help during lift-off, while maneuvering in space, with flying back into the earth's atmosphere, and with landing the shuttle on the ground. Separate booster rockets attached to the shuttle during launching help with lift-off from earth, then separate and fall away. The shuttle would also need a team of pilots and mission specialists to begin studying the chances of space travel for extended periods of time.

Ellison Onizuka was one of 220 out of 8,100 astronaut candidates selected to be interviewed by NASA officials. His top physical condition, excellent engineering background, and confident but friendly personality impressed the members of the interviewing panel. He became one of the final thirty-five men and women astronauts chosen for NASA's space shuttle program.

In 1978, the Onizukas moved to Houston, Texas, where Ellison would begin training at the Johnson Space Center. Pilots and mission specialists took classes in astronomy, oceanography, computers, and mathematics. They trained and practiced in simulated weightless atmospheres, lift-off, and landing procedures. As a mission specialist, Ellison received additional training in his technical assignments, and in confidential projects for the Department of Defense. Part of his responsibilities as an astronaut also included speaking to community and school groups and giving interviews to newspapers, television, and radio.

An astronaut's schedule leaves little free time. However, Ellison Onizuka always made time for his family. Janelle and Darien were both enthusiastic soccer players. Their father served as a chapter member and officer of the soccer booster club and attended as many games as

Onizuka at astronaut training school, Vance Air Force Base, Oklahoma, 1978

possible, cheering his daughters on to victory. His interest in 4-H continued as he and Lorna became members of the Livestock Show and Rodeo International Committee. Whenever he had time left over for his own relaxation, Ellison would spend it deep-sea fishing.

Astronauts were selected from the original group of thirty-five to fly the different space shuttle missions. In 1982, Onizuka was chosen along with four other astronauts to participate in a secret shuttle mission for the Department of Defense. During this mission, communications between the ground and crew, as well as the activities conducted on board during the flight, would not be made public even after landing. The exact launch date was kept confidential and was postponed for over two years from the original date. Finally, on January 24, 1985, the crew of the *Discovery* accelerated toward outer space, going from zero to 25,600 feet per second in just eight and one-half minutes. Ellison took special mementos with him, which included Kona coffee and macadamia nuts to drink and eat, the Buddhist medallion that his father had given him, and patches from the Japanese-American 442nd Combat Team and the 100th Battalion whose wartime courage and loyalty he greatly admired.

The *Discovery*'s mission lasted three days, and the return to earth was safe and smooth. Lt. Col. Ellison Onizuka became the first Asian American in space and a hero to Japanese Americans across the United States. In the months following the flight of *Discovery*, Ellison Onizuka made numerous public appearances, especially in his home state of Hawaii. When he returned home to Kona, Ellison took the time to visit his family, friends, and the people who helped him to accomplish his career dream. He also made sure that more than half of his engagements were always reserved for speaking to students in schools.

By early 1985, upon completion of the *Discovery* flight, Ellison Onizuka knew he had been selected as part of *Challenger*'s seven-person crew. This flight was scheduled for late January, 1986, and would not be a secret military mission. This crew represented six different religions, three ethnic groups, seven home states, both men and women, military and nonmilitary personnel, and seven

Mission Specialist Onizuka of the Challenger *crew, 1986*

areas of expertise: pilot, copilot, electrical engineer, aerospace engineer, laser physicist, satellite communications designer, and teacher. On a cold January morning, each crew member boarded *Challenger* with excited anticipation. Friends and family were in the viewing stands at Kennedy Space Center in Florida, ready to witness another historic lift-off into space. Seventy-three seconds after lift-off, a malfunctioning rocket booster caused an explosion aboard the *Challenger* that abruptly ended the flight in tragedy.

Astronaut Ellison Onizuka has left behind wonderful memories of a person dedicated to his family, his career, and his dream. He would choose to be remembered by young readers through the message he delivered to Konawaena High School's graduating class in 1980:

> "If I can impress on you only one idea tonight, let it be that the people who make this world run, whose lives can be termed successful, whose names will go down in the history books are not the cynics, the critics, or the armchair quarterbacks.
>
> "They are the adventurers, the explorers, and doers of this world. When they see a wrong or a problem, they do something about it. When they see a vacant place in our knowledge, they work to fill that void.
>
> "Rather than leaning back and criticizing how things are, they work to make things the way they should be. They are the aggressive, the self-starter, the innovative, and the imaginative of this world.
>
> "Every generation has the obligation to free men's

minds for a look at new worlds . . . to look out from a higher plateau than the last generation.

"Your vision is not limited by what your eye can see, but by what your mind can imagine. Many things that you take for granted were considered unrealistic dreams by previous generations. If you accept these past accomplishments as commonplace, then think of the new horizons that you can explore.

"From your vantage point, your education and imagination will carry you to places which you won't believe possible.

"Make your life count—and the world will be a better place because you tried."

I. M. Pei

 The Rock and Roll Hall of Fame had already honored legends such as the Beatles, Elvis Presley, Mick Jagger, and the Beach Boys, but it had no museum to pay respect to its inductees. The Louvre in Paris had been a palace for kings before its doors were thrown open to the public during the French Revolution. Nearly two hundred years later, the French president wanted the historic museum enlarged and modernized while maintaining a monumental appearance. Towering at seventy-two stories, a bank in Hong Kong is Asia's tallest building. I. M. Pei was chosen to design each project. As one of the world's leading architects, Mr. Pei has also solved problems of low-cost city housing.

I. M. Pei's father had wanted him to become a doctor, but the son was sickened by blood. The teen-ager was interested in architecture and has said that he decided to study in the United States because he liked American movies. He started at the University of Pennsylvania but, worried that his architectural drawing ability was not good enough for that type of program, he switched to engineering at the Massachusetts Institute of Technology (MIT). Ultimately, he returned to the study of architecture and continued his studies at Harvard University.

For over forty-five years, Mr. Pei's career has flourished. He has designed many buildings in the United States and in foreign countries, sparking interest, admiration, and sometimes controversy. Originally, he wanted to practice in his homeland, but world events altered his plans.

Tsuyee and Lien Kwun Chwong Pei's eldest son was born in the Year of the Snake, on April 26, 1917, in Canton, China. He was named Ieoh Ming, which means "to inscribe brightly." Tsuyee Pei headed a regional branch of the Bank of China in Canton and then in Hong Kong before settling his family in Shanghai in 1927. He was in charge of the bank's Shanghai office, and sent his ten-year-old son to prestigious St. John's Middle School. The boy studied in an international atmosphere. The Pei family also owned a grand house with a magnificent garden in Suzhou, a nearby resort, and they spent weekends and holidays there. This was a very happy period of Ieoh Ming's life, until his mother became ill and died.

Shanghai experienced much construction during these years. Young Ieoh Ming watched buildings rise in his city, and became keenly interested in architecture. Many wealthy Chinese sent their children to college abroad,

I. M. Pei

and Ieoh Ming went to the United States. He arrived at
the University of Pennsylvania in 1935, but soon trans-
ferred to MIT where he felt more comfortable with its
practical, structural engineering approach. MIT had
many other Chinese students, and Ieoh Ming joined F.F.,
a Chinese fraternity. The young architectural student soon
became known by his initials, I.M.
During the summer of 1938, he worked for an architectural firm in New York City. One of his MIT fraternity
brothers introduced him to Eileen Loo. Her father had
also been educated at MIT. She had just arrived from
Hong Kong to begin college at Wellesley, not far from
MIT. I.M. offered to drive Eileen to Boston, but she
declined, since they had just met. Over the next few
years, they dated. I.M. graduated in 1940, and married
Eileen a day before she received her degree in 1942.

I. M. Pei enrolled in the Harvard Graduate School of
Design in 1942, but six months later he left to help with
the American war effort. He worked with the National
Defense Research Committee in Princeton, New Jersey,
using his knowledge of construction. Just before World
War II ended, he returned to Harvard, where Eileen had
been studying landscape architecture. He studied under
architects Walter Gropius and Marcel Breuer, and taught
at Harvard before and after receiving his master's degree
in architecture from its Graduate School of Design in
1946.

Mr. Pei left university life in 1948. He had drawn
some original designs, but had not yet built anything.
When real estate developer William Zeckendorf saw some

of Mr. Pei's sketches, he was very impressed and hired him as Director of Architecture at the large firm of Webb & Knapp, Inc. From then on, I. M. Pei had the chance to plan and build many projects, such as apartments, shopping centers, and offices. He also learned how to complete his assignments on time and on a budget. Mr. Pei has said that looking through the eyes of a developer was a valuable experience to him as an architect. He understood the importance of context, how a building fits into its surroundings. Transportation and nearby properties had to be considered. Mr. Pei also realized how clients must trust an architect, and the responsibility an architect has in affecting an area and those who live or work there.

When I. M. Pei's and Eileen Loo's parents had sent their children to be educated in the United States, they expected them to later return and work in China. The events of World War II and the victory of the Communists in China changed those plans. In 1954, both Ieoh Ming and Eileen Pei became American citizens. They already had three sons, T'ing Chung, Chien Chung, and Li Chung, all named by Mr. Pei's father, who himself moved to New York after World War II. In 1960, a daughter, Liane, was born. The Peis were anxious for the children to become assimilated and to blend into American life. They were not taught to speak Chinese, a decision Mr. Pei says he since regrets.

By 1955, I. M. Pei was ready to start his own firm. He has earned a reputation for his modern designs with geometric shapes, his ability to combine the old and new, and his determination to relate each project to its surroundings. The National Center for Atmospheric Research in Boulder, Colorado, with its reddish towers appearing to be part of the mountainous scenery, gained him early national attention. The design was begun in 1961 and completed in 1967, an average amount of time for many of Mr. Pei's projects. During the 1960s, a variety of assignments included the Luce Memorial Chapel in Taiwan, a terminal at John F. Kennedy Airport in New York City, and a plan for the business district of Oklahoma City. For redevelopment in the Bedford-Stuyvesant section of Brooklyn, he worked to revitalize the streets and neighborhood with designs for two reconfigured superblocks. Also in New York City, Mr. Pei involved community leaders to help with expansion plans for Columbia University, since the surrounding neighbors as well as the school would be affected.

One project that did not go so well for I. M. Pei & Partners was the glass-sheathed John Hancock Building in Boston. The skyscraper was enthusiastically received as it was being built in the early 1970s. However, before construction was complete, the pale blue sheets of glass, part of the "curtain-wall," began falling out. Accusations were made and lawsuits filed. The architects blamed the manufacturer. The troublesome double-paned windows were replaced with more conventional single panes. Business for the Pei firm fell sharply. Yet as the highrise was repaired, public confidence began to return, and Mr. Pei's office was yet to design some of its most famous works.

The East Building of the National Gallery of Art in

Washington, D.C., presented a unique set of challenges. The original National Gallery was a neoclassical style, visually similar to many of that city's historical buildings, even though it had been completed as recently as 1941. The new wing was to be built on a very visible lot in Washington. The site was bounded by the grassy Mall, which stretches from the Capitol past the Washington Monument to the Lincoln Memorial. Mr. Pei has said that he wanted a contemporary design, but one that would look well near the more traditional styles. He was careful to consider the height of his building and used neighboring structures as guides. The master plan for the Mall area dated back to 1791, and Mr. Pei felt a great responsibility. The East Building was aligned with the original National Gallery, joined underneath but separated at ground level by a cobblestone plaza. For his building, Mr. Pei used the same pink Tennessee marble that was used for the original Gallery. It was from the same quarries and even chosen by the same man who had selected the marble decades earlier, although he had since retired. Planning began in 1968, construction started in 1971, and the project was completed in 1978. Mr. Pei was the firm's partner in charge, but many other architects, including his second son, Chien Chung, were also involved. The finished complex boasts a waterfall which looks like a wall of water because it begins outside but is visible indoors through glass at a lower level. The center of the wing has a skylit roof formed by twenty-five glass tetrahedrons. The interior spaces of the building are also geometrically shaped and angled. Outside, several glass pyramids rise from the plaza, an image that soon would be associated with Mr. Pei in a European capital city as well as America's.

French President François Mitterrand admired the East Building of the National Gallery of Art in Washington, D.C. He appreciated Mr. Pei's ability to compliment the old with the new. In 1982, he chose the architect for a similar but much grander and more difficult assignment in Paris. Construction of the Louvre began in the year 1202. Originally, it was a fortified castle, but later became a palace for French kings. After the French Revolution, the once royal residence became one of the world's greatest art museums, housing such masterpieces as Leonardo da Vinci's *Mona Lisa*. In present times, over three million people come to the Louvre each year; however, it had never been built as a museum. More space was necessary for museum services. The awkward flow of visitors in the U-shaped building needed change. While the museum would be expanded and updated, it was essential not to interfere with its historic image.

Mr. Pei employed ingenious solutions to the job's many hurdles. As excavation began, walls of the original castle were uncovered, and they became an exhibition. The Louvre was enlarged underground, beneath its huge court. The entrance was moved from one side to the center. This time, a glass pyramid seventy-one feet high beckoned in the plaza while illuminating the reception area below. Special, clear glass was chosen for the panels of the pyramid, not ordinary glass which has a slight green tint. The enormous glass and steel structure is a

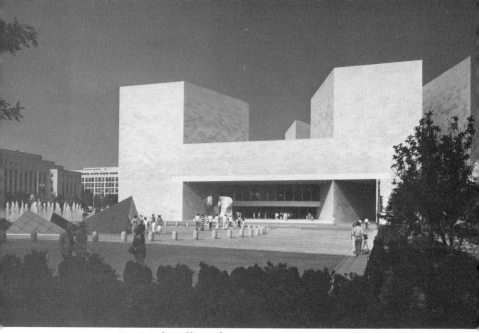

ABOVE: *National Gallery of Art, East Building, Washington, D.C.*

BELOW: *The Grand Louvre, Paris*

modern touch which still permits a view of the revered building. Initially, public reaction was mixed, as some French people disagreed with the mixing of architectural styles and resented the change in their Louvre. However, by July, 1989, the end of the first phase of the Grand Louvre project, even most critics embraced Mr. Pei's pyramid as it was becoming a famous monument itself.

Mr. Pei's firm would work on a number of projects at the same time. While the Grand Louvre was progressing, Mr. Pei also designed the Bank of China branch in Hong Kong, now known as the People's Republic's international bank. He felt especially proud of the skyscraper, with its glass facade arranged in a pattern of triangles, because years ago his father had founded that branch of the bank. That high-rise is the tallest building in all of Asia.

The firm changed its name to Pei Cobb Freed & Partners in 1989. The company is very large, with over two hundred employees. Most of the employees are architects, two of them I. M. Pei's sons. Chien Chung Pei was a member of the teams which worked on the East Building of the National Gallery and on the Louvre. He and his French fiancee chose to be married in Paris the week the Grand Louvre was opened because the Pei family would already be in that city for the museum celebrations. Li Chung Pei was part of the bank project in Hong Kong. The Peis' eldest son is a real estate developer, while their daughter is an attorney.

When Mr. Pei was asked to design the Rock and Roll Hall of Fame and Museum, he was very surprised. He admitted that he was not a fan of rock and roll. He had always instructed his children to lower the volume on such music. He said that he preferred classical music, and was even working on a symphony hall in Dallas. That did not matter and, in 1987, Mr. Pei was still selected. He planned the Cleveland, Ohio, attraction to include performance and exhibit spaces, a music and film library, listening rooms, a tower rising to two hundred feet, and one of his famous glass atriums. Mr. Pei has said he did not have to persuade people from the firm to work on the project. All those who loved rock and roll were very eager. One of the other architects even made tape recordings of some rock classics, so that Mr. Pei could become more familiar with the music. I. M. Pei soon appreciated the Beatles, Chuck Berry, and early Bob Dylan. He then went to concerts by Paul Simon and Genesis, and enjoyed a dazzling performance by Little Richard.

The Rock and Roll Hall of Fame is only a recent example of I. M. Pei's dedication to his work. He has designed many different projects all over the world, for all kinds of clients, but he approaches each new job with a sense of great responsibility. Just as he had to preserve the eight-hundred-year-old walls discovered deep inside the Louvre before he could proceed with that project, I. M. Pei had to understand rock and roll before he could build its monument. With his concern, attention to detail, and memorable geometric shapes, Mr. Pei has given the world some of its most innovative architecture.

Samuel C. C. Ting

 Deep in the earth, under portions of France and Switzerland, stretches an enormous tunnel. It crosses the French-Swiss border four times as it forms a circle sweeping seventeen miles around. This is not an ordinary tunnel, built for cars or trains, but one which will help answer basic scientific questions about weight and mass. A detector, several stories high, sits nearly one hundred feet deep, ready to measure tiny subatomic particles which collide at its center. For now, this new accelerator is the largest in the world, and it is also the heart of a massive scientific experiment.

The project is based at the European Organization for Nuclear Research, known as CERN, in Geneva, Switzerland, and has attracted hundreds of scientists from many countries. Many commute regularly from other jobs,

Dr. Samuel C. C. Ting, a winner of the Nobel Prize in Physics, 1976

thousands of miles away. "I cross the Atlantic forty times a year," says Dr. Samuel C. C. Ting, who oversees the project and travels from the Massachusetts Institute of Technology (MIT). Dr. Ting has been making these trips for years. He is one of the leaders in the field of particle physics and the winner of a Nobel Prize.

Dr. Ting has been interested in science since he was a child, although he did not attend school until he was twelve. Samuel Chao Chung Ting was born in Ann Arbor, Michigan, on January 27, 1936. He would be the eldest of three children for Kuan Hai Ting and Jeanne M. Wong Ting. At the time of Samuel's birth, his parents were both professors at the University of Michigan in Ann Arbor, his father in engineering and his mother in psychology. Just three months after Samuel was born, the family returned to China. However, there were wartime conditions there, and for years the family lived like refugees as they fled from place to place. Dr. Ting says that his family always had enough food and shelter, but otherwise he was on his own. He had no formal schooling or organized sports. "I was not taught by my parents. It was during wartime. My parents were university professors, busy by themselves, so I was self-taught." Though young Samuel had no real teachers, he enjoyed meeting scholars who often visited his parents, and he realizes he was very lucky to know such people. "Both my parents were quite interested in science," he says, but he credits his grandmother for sparking his curiosity with stories of famous scientific discoveries and the people involved. "My mother's mother brought me up and told me about Michael Faraday and Isaac Newton. This was more important than anything else."

In 1948, the Tings went to Taiwan. The island had recently been returned to China, after being occupied by Japan for fifty years. Dr. Ting recalls that education was very important and that the school system was very strict.

He first started school in a small town, and then the family moved to Taipei, the capital. He had to take an exam to enroll in that city's finest high school. He passed and was even put in the best class, although he admits that he was not the best student in all subjects. Samuel was not particularly good in either English or Chinese literature, he suspects, because of his late start in school. During high school, his main interest was Chinese history, and he also enjoyed physics and chemistry. He decided to further concentrate in science, as he realized it was easier to determine truth in science than in history. Also, he could truly focus on physics and chemistry and felt he was developing a great understanding of those subjects. Samuel was a serious student, but also took time for other activities, such as biking. "When I was young in Taiwan, I rode a bike around the island. It took two weeks," he remembers.

After graduating from high school in 1956, Samuel chose engineering at the University of Michigan. He returned to his birthplace, Ann Arbor, but he knew very little English. His first year was especially difficult when he started college. He had received a scholarship, and he had to work very hard and earn good grades to keep it. The following year, he switched his major to physics in order to take more advanced courses in math, physics, and physical chemistry. Also, he had decided that he really wanted to concentrate in physics, which is the science of energy and matter and their interaction. Physics can involve the study of light, heat, sound, electricity, magnetism, radiation, and atomic structure. Although

Samuel still had some difficulty with English, he was eager to ask questions when he did not understand a concept, and also to gain a deeper knowledge of the subject. Looking back, Dr. Ting recognizes a pattern in his college work. He says that scientists must go beyond what is taught in textbooks and they must think independently. Also, they cannot hesitate to ask questions, even when their view may be unpopular. Still remembering his college days, Dr. Ting says, "At the University of Michigan, I went to all the football games. I still go back."

Samuel Ting earned his bachelor and doctoral degrees at Michigan in just six years. He received many fine job offers when he completed his doctorate in 1962, but he did not select the one with the highest salary. Instead, he chose to take a one-year position at CERN in Geneva, Switzerland, with a Ford Foundation Fellowship. He worked on a particle accelerator. Accelerators are used in the research of subatomic particles, the tiny components of an atom. Accelerators are large devices that force certain particles to reach very high speeds and energies. These high-speed particles are made to collide with a specific target or with one another. Detectors register information about the particles' collisions. Most acclerators have very long paths because the particles, as they travel, lose more energy and speed in tight turns.

Dr. Ting then became an instructor at Columbia University in New York City. He was very impressed by the physics department, which included several Nobel Prize winners. While at Columbia, he learned of an interesting

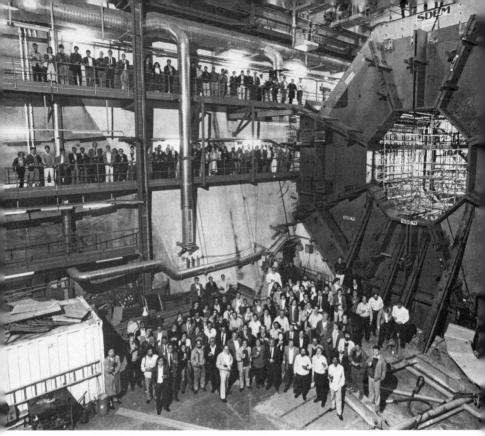

Scientists appear tiny next to the detector under construction at CERN in 1987. Dr. Ting is at bottom left.

experiment being conducted on an accelerator at Harvard University. Its results seemed to contradict some widely believed predictions. Dr. Ting became curious and wanted to repeat the experiment, although some senior professors were not encouraging. They did not believe the experiment would prove successful and they did not think that Dr. Ting had enough experience to do the work. Dr. Ting was finally permitted to take a leave of absence in Germany to conduct the research, although one senior professor still bet him twenty dollars that he would not finish his work in three years. After only eight months, Dr. Ting's group finished the experiment, proved the initial theoretical predictions had indeed been correct, and Dr. Ting won his twenty dollars. This experiment also proved to be the beginning of a path that led to his Nobel Prize.

In 1967, Dr. Ting accepted a position at the Massachusetts Institute of Technology (MIT). By this time, he and his first wife had two young daughters, Jeanne and Amy. In 1969, he was promoted to full professor at MIT. Dr. Ting says that within a few years he realized there might be subatomic particles with the properties of light rays, yet with a heavier mass. At an accelerator at Brookhaven National Laboratory on Long Island in New York, Dr. Ting and his colleagues began to search for these heavier mass photons. Although such photons were not predicted by theory, he just felt there was no reason why they could not exist. The scientists designed a detector to search for heavy mass photons with a long lifetime. They encountered criticism because the experiment was very expensive and it was believed that even if such heavy mass photons did exist, their lifetime would be short and less costly equipment could be used. Also, a similar experiment had already been conducted and no long-life photons had been found. However, once again Dr. Ting was persistent and was not discouraged.

In August, 1974, Dr. Ting and his team at Brookhaven first saw evidence of a new and unpredicted particle, just what they wanted to find. The results were checked and double-checked over several months. Physicists from a laboratory in Italy were able to confirm Dr. Ting's findings and articles were prepared to announce the discovery to the world. About the same time, in November, 1974, Dr. Ting visited the Stanford Linear Accelerator Center (SLAC) in California. He described his exciting news, only to learn that a SLAC physicist he knew, Dr. Burton Richter, had just reported similar results. As the two men discussed their work, they realized that independently each had discovered the same particle. Dr. Ting called the particle "J" while Dr. Richter had chosen the name "psi." The two papers announcing the new particle, one from Brookhaven and the other from Stanford, were published simultaneously.

Dr. Ting feels that the discovery of the J/psi particle, as it became known, was very important because physicists realized their knowledge of elementary particles was not complete. The existence of J/psi meant that there were probably other new particles, yet undiscovered. Finding J/psi led to a worldwide pursuit of finding new particles, and Dr. Ting says it changed the way scientists understand subatomic physics.

Dr. Ting was conducting research at CERN in Switzerland when he learned he had won the 1976 Nobel Prize in Physics with Dr. Richter. The great honor, awarded in Sweden, came only two years after their discoveries. Such quick recognition is unusual. The two men shared the award worth $162,140. Dr. Ting laughs when he says how the Nobel Prize changed his life. "It is easier to get grants!" He adds, more seriously, "It allowed easier access to people and things, but it has not changed my research." For students considering a scientific career, he advises, "If you go into science, you must realize you are doing it for your own interest, not glory or fame. There is no guarantee of that. You need hard work and also luck. You must think science is most important. If you do the work for fame, you will be disappointed."

The Nobel Prize is just one of many honors and awards from around the world for Dr. Ting. His other distinctions include honorary professorships at two schools in China, six honorary doctorates from universities around the world, membership in the National Academy of Science in the United States, and foreign memberships in both the Soviet and Pakistan Academies of Science, and Academia Sinica (Taiwan). Dr. Ting has also received the Ernest Orlando Lawrence Award from the United States government and the De Gasperi Gold Medal in Science from the Italian Republic. As part of his responsibilities in the scientific community, Dr. Ting publishes numerous articles in professional journals which describe his work. He is also on the editorial boards of several journals.

Dr. Ting is one of the most celebrated physicists in the world, but he willingly shares some of his own thoughts on his life as a physicist, and even some personal doubts. He says he always picked a topic of great interest to him. Even though, at times, probability or opinion was against his views or experimental plans, he still carried out his work. Dr. Ting makes sure that he checks and rechecks all his work, saying he has always questioned his results and capabilities. He says he has always thought he had limited ability, but felt that perhaps he could make a scientific contribution by working extremely hard and excelling in a specific area.

In the years since the Nobel Prize, Dr. Ting has con-

Dr. Samuel Ting, 1987. Equations for the Higgs boson are on the blackboard behind him.

tinued at MIT, while still routinely flying to CERN in Switzerland. His brother, John, is an engineer in New Jersey, and his sister, Susan, lives in New Jersey. His daughters are now grown, but they are not scientists. "They are independent. Both are artists," he updates. In 1985, he married Dr. Susan Marks. Their son, Christopher, was born a year later. The family lives in Geneva, though Dr. Ting travels regularly to MIT. He adds, "For Christmas, we all come back." Dr. Ting has little free time, but says, "I like to swim and watch football," particularly mentioning the University of Michigan games.

Dr. Samuel Ting continues to search for new particles, especially a type of subatomic particle called the Higgs boson, named after Scottish physicist Peter Higgs. With their underground detector in Europe, he and other scientists are trying to find this particle, even though they are not sure it exists. If found, the Higgs could explain why objects have weight in a gravitational field. Scientists think the actions of the Higgs create mass as other particles interact with it. At the project beneath part of the French-Swiss border, subatomic particles will speed through the seventeen-mile-long tunnel which makes this new accelerator the largest yet built. The particles will collide at the center of the detector, and its instruments will measure the resulting particles. Even if the Higgs exists, its life would be so short that it could not be seen directly, but the complex detector could still relay information about its existence and properties. The discovery would be a major one, and could provide answers to age-old questions about the laws of physical science.

An Wang

In 1951, Dr. An Wang began his company, Wang Laboratories, with $600 in savings, no contracts, orders, or office furniture, and one determined, full-time employee—himself. Since then, through the development and sales of electronic calculators, word processors, and office automation systems, Wang Labs has become a company with sales of $2.4 billion and about 20,000 employees on its payroll. Dr. Wang was recognized as one of the richest men in the United States, yet he lived a quiet, simple life, never owning more than two suits at a time.

Dr. Wang had said that his success came from the confidence that he developed at an early age. An Wang, whose name means "Peaceful King," was born on February 7, 1920, in Shanghai, China, the oldest son of five children. Growing up during a period of Chinese history called the "Age of Confusion," An Wang witnessed the struggles between the ruling warlords, the Nationalists, and the Communists, and later, the Japanese invasion of China. During this time, he was often required to take on more responsibilities than other children his age. From these experiences, An Wang discovered that he could make decisions and accomplish tasks that surprised many adults.

When An Wang was six years old, his family moved to Kun San, a city about thirty miles north of Shanghai where his father taught English in a private elementary school. This was young An's first opportunity to learn how to deal with difficult situations. He was to attend his father's school and, since there were no lower grade classes, young An was enrolled as a third grader. For the rest of his schooling in China, he was two years younger than his classmates. Later, in his autobiography, *Lessons*, An Wang recalled that even though he did not choose to begin third grade at the age of six, he could handle the work and get along with his peers. He said it felt like "being thrown in the water when you don't know how to swim. You either learn how to swim—and fast— or you sink!"

An remembered that math came easy to him, while other subjects such as history or geography were difficult. He enjoyed spending his afternoons reading at the public library and was especially impressed by the biographies about Western leaders of science, such as Leonardo da Vinci, Galileo, and Isaac Newton. In addition to his daily schooling, young An's grandmother gave him lessons in

Portrait of Dr. An Wang

Chinese literature and Confucian thought. Confucius was an ancient Chinese philosopher, whose teachings included devotion to family and friends and keeping peace and justice. According to An Wang, his success in business and his belief in serving the community were related to the ancient philosopher's ideas of moderation, patience, balance, and simplicity.

In junior high and high school, An Wang continued to excel in the areas of math and science. At that time in Kun San, there were not enough public junior high schools to serve the great number of students who wished to attend. Admission was based on the scores of a highly competitive examination where less than 200 students with top scores and grades were accepted. An was disadvantaged by being two years younger, but felt confident that he would do well on the exam. An was admitted to junior high, having achieved the highest test scores of any applicant. At thirteen years old, An started Shanghai Provincial High School, considered to be one of the best high schools in China. When the school relocated ten miles out of Shanghai, An moved away from home to live on the school's campus. Many of his courses were taught in English and he used several of the same textbooks that American students used during their first year of college. Although students were required to learn English from the fourth grade, studying high school subjects in English was difficult. Later, when An went to the United States to study, he realized that his high school had prepared him well.

An Wang entered Chiao Tung University in Shanghai

at the age of sixteen, majoring in electrical engineering and specializing in communications. He enjoyed his two favorite subjects, math and physics, and found the work to be easy. When he was not studying, he carried out the duties of class president, an office he held for four years, and competed on the university's table tennis team. An Wang recalled that being younger than his classmates, he was at a size disadvantage when playing team sports. Whenever he played soccer in high school, he felt more like the "target" than the goalie. However, he did not become discouraged, and discovered the sport of table tennis where size was not such an important factor.

At Chiao Tung University, An Wang participated in several projects. Having founded a student newspaper in junior high, he continued his interest in publishing by translating scientific articles from English into Chinese. He read through *Popular Mechanics* and *Popular Science* to find interesting magazine articles reflecting new ideas and technology from the West. During his college years, World War II was raging throughout Europe, and Shanghai was invaded by Japanese troops. The university was moved into a nearby "international zone" governed by the French which was, for a period of time, safe from the Japanese. An Wang graduated from the university and continued on in the year following as a teaching assistant in electrical engineering. With eight of his classmates, he volunteered for a project that would take him deep into mainland China to the town of Kweilin. Their job was to design and build radios and transmitters for the Central Radio Corporation, which served the Chinese government troops. Kweilin was not untouched by the war. Weekly bombing raids sent An and the team of engineers to the safety of deep hillside caverns where they would wait out the attacks playing the card game of bridge. While working on this project, An Wang learned of his father's death. He was still recovering from the news of his mother's death a few years earlier.

He was now on his own and after the end of the war, An Wang had the opportunity to be one of hundreds of Chinese engineers selected to study American technology. The purpose of this two-year program was to prepare trained engineers for the rebuilding of war-torn China. For some of his colleagues, this would be their first exposure to Western culture, but An had a head start. He had learned English from his father and, in school, studied from American textbooks, read about Western scientists and technology, and enjoyed American films such as *Gone with the Wind* and movies about the Wild West. Arriving in Washington, D.C., in 1945 brought an unexpected turn of events.

While waiting for his assignment to an American company, An Wang decided that he could learn more as a graduate student than an observer. He applied to Harvard University, was accepted in September of 1945, and earned his master's degree in the following year. After a brief clerical job with the Chinese government supply agency in Ottawa, Canada, he returned to Harvard in 1947 and began the Ph.D. program in physics. During the 1940s, computer science was just beginning to emerge and, although An Wang's graduate work was

A new student at Harvard University

somewhat related, he did not earn his doctorate degree in this specific field. He was awarded his Ph.D. before the end of 1948.

In the spring of 1948, Dr. Wang became a research assistant in the Harvard Computation Laboratory. His work with Dr. Howard Aiken, a pioneer in computer development, eventually led An Wang to establish Wang Laboratories. Dr. Aiken designed one of the first computers to operate in the United States, called the Mark I. In spite of its large size, filling almost an entire room, small amount of memory for data storage, and high noise level when it was running, the Mark I was considered to be a major breakthrough in the development of the modern computer. Dr. Aiken presented Dr. Wang with the problem of increasing the speed at which the computer can access stored information, now called memory. After much trial and error, Dr. Wang solved this problem by inventing "memory cores." These memory cores allowed programs and data to be stored inside the computer itself, increasing the rate at which information or data could be used. In addition, this invention made it possible for the computer to work with simpler computer "languages," which eventually expanded usage to a more general population.

During the time that An Wang was working as a research assistant, he met Lorraine Chiu at a social get-together for Chinese students and professionals. Lorraine was from Shanghai, where she graduated from St. John's College before coming to the Boston area to pursue graduate studies in English literature at Wellesley College. The young couple was married a year after they met, but without her parent's approval. Communication was difficult at that time because of the civil war in China, forcing them to break from this marriage tradition. The Wangs have three children, Frederick, Courtney, and Juliette. Their two sons later became a part of Wang Laboratories. Fred has worked in different departments of the company and is now a member of the Board of Directors. Courtney is a vice-president and also a member of the company's Board.

In the early 1950s, the Harvard Computation Labo-

Lorraine Wang, wife, and daughter, Juliette

ratory began to move away from computer research. Dr. Wang decided to patent his invention and to start Wang Laboratories by selling memory cores and contracting with industry to do special computer technology projects. The electronic scoreboard at Shea Stadium in New York and the LINASEC, which was the first electronic system to set type in even columns for newspapers, as well as the sale of the memory core patent to IBM, contributed to the growth of Wang Laboratories. It was not until the introduction of their new product, the desktop calculator, that Wang Laboratories quickly developed into a million dollar business employing over four hundred people by 1967.

In 1965, the first of two desktop calculator models was presented, the LOCI (logarithmic calculating instrument) with a price tag of $6,500. It could add, subtract, multiply, compute square roots, and do calculations that scientists and engineers needed in their work. The LOCI performed calculations that were more difficult than addition or subtraction. Since this calculator was faster and could do calculations that surpassed other calculators on the market, a patent was awarded to Dr. Wang for the LOCI. Less than a year after the LOCI was marketed, the Model 300 desktop calculator was introduced. The Model 300 was easier to use and cost $1,695. With the Model 300, sales increased dramatically in the United States, as well as in newly established Wang Labs offices in Belgium, Taiwan, and the United Kingdom. Desktop calculators were eventually replaced by the modern and very inexpensive "pocket" calculators of today.

With the increasing changes in technology, Dr. Wang decided to begin work on a new project. He believed that there was a growing market for inexpensive, "general-purpose" minicomputers that could be programmed to fit any user's needs. The first minicomputer that Wang Laboratories developed was the Model 700, and it was also the last to use memory cores for storage of data. The models following the 700 replaced memory cores with new technology, random access memory (RAM) chips, which did the same job as the memory cores but were much smaller in size. The sales of the Wang minicomputers were not as successful as the desktop calculators, which maintained their popularity. However, the company continued to grow and by 1970, sales increased to over $25 million, and the number of employees to almost fifteen hundred people.

Looking at the developing needs of the business world in the 1970s led Dr. Wang to design a computer system that would make the secretary's job much easier. The first word-processing typewriter, the 1200, was introduced at the end of 1971. The 1200 enabled the secretary to type a letter and correct any mistakes line-by-line before printing a final copy. The system was also capable of storing all parts of the letter to be used again through special signals recorded on cassette tape and then played back to the word processor. Dr. Wang noted that the average secretary was working at the rate of less than eighteen words per minute when typing the final copy of a 250-word business letter. With the 1200, a finished copy of the same business letter could be printed at 175 words per minute.

In 1976, Wang Laboratories presented a revolutionary new word-processing system called WPS. Before the WPS, moving words or correcting mistakes could be accomplished only a few lines at a time and only one line of the document could be seen at a time. The new system allowed the office worker to view the entire document on a large CRT (cathode ray tube) screen, which resembles a television screen. Words or sentences could be moved or corrected from any part of the document appearing on the CRT screen. In addition, through a series of "menus," directions in simple language could be given to guide the secretary when using the WPS. Dr. Wang recalled that at the word-processing show where the WPS was first demonstrated, the people stood almost ten deep and soon invitations needed to be given to keep the crowd under control. He remembered that when the people saw words and sentences being moved and edited on a large screen, they "thought it was magic." The next step for Wang Laboratories was to bring word-processing systems and minicomputers together to serve the needs of a particular business and increase production by saving time. This was accomplished through Wang's Office Information Systems (OIS). With OIS, information could be processed by secretaries, sales people, or managers through just one system, rather than each group using a separate computer or word processor.

Since the beginning of Wang Laboratories in the early 1950s, Dr. Wang's goal was to provide workers with equipment and services to make their jobs easier. Equally important to Dr. Wang was the well-being of his employees and customers, as well as "giving-back" to the community and society. Wang Laboratories employees respected him for his intellect, his style of "leading by example," his willingness to provide employees with a way to express their ideas or problems. He made a special effort to personally visit almost fifty U.S. and eight international sales offices during the mid-1980s when computer sales were down. He listened to customer complaints about the sales and service of Wang's equipment, and used this information to improve business operations. Some of his community contributions have been to help restore Boston's performing arts theater, the Wang Center; to become a major funder of the Massachusetts General Hospital outpatient clinic, serving close to 500,000 people a year; to donate a Wang computer network system to New York City's center for the homeless. Additionally, Dr. Wang has funded scholarships and student exchange programs with mainland China that he felt would promote a "better understanding of Chinese culture." He was awarded the Medal of Liberty by the U.S. government, along with eleven others born in other countries and who, as American citizens, have made important contributions.

Over the years, Wang Laboratories has been able to weather the changes that come with a growing business. It was Dr. Wang's hope that the leadership team will keep Wang Laboratories growing and successful to continue competing with industry giants, like IBM. On March 24, 1990, Dr. Wang lost his battle with cancer of the esophagus. He will be remembered as a visionary businessman, an inventor who held over forty patents, and someone who was dedicated to giving more to the world than what he had been given at birth.

Selected Bibliography

Personal or telephone interviews were made by the authors with many of the subjects in this book. In several cases, assistants or family members were consulted.

JOSE ARUEGO

Appel, Ida J. and Turkish, Marion P. "Profile: The Magic World of Jose Aruego." *Language Arts*, May, 1977.

Raymond, Allen. "Jose Aruego: From Law Books to Kids' Books." *Teaching K-8*, August/September, 1987.

MICHAEL CHANG

Bonk, Thomas. "Chang Breaks Hip in Freak Mishap." *Los Angeles Times*, December 9, 1989.

Bonk, Thomas. "Boy Wonder." *Los Angeles Times Magazine*, August 27, 1989.

Kirkpatrick, Curry. "Giant Killers." *Sports Illustrated*, June 19, 1989.

CONNIE CHUNG

Appelo, Tim. "Anchors Aweigh." *Savvy*, April, 1988.

Sandroff, Ronni; MacIntosh, Claire; and Russell, Anne M. "Career Workshop" and "How to Get the Job You Really Want." *Working Woman*, April, 1989.

Stoner, Kevin R. and Donahue, Hugh Carter. "Journalistic Reality . . ." *Broadcasting*, January, 1990.

Zoglin, Richard. "Star Wars at the Networks." *Time*, April 3, 1989.

MYUNG-WHUN CHUNG

Cariaga, Daniel. "Myung-Whun Chung." *Los Angeles Times*, September 1, 1978.

Crutchfield, Will. "A Sudden Ascent to the Top in Opera." *The New York Times*, May 25, 1989.

Kim, Rose. "Storming the Bastille." *Transpacific*, November/ December, 1989.

Riding, Alan. "At the Bastille Opera Chung Is Finally Free to Face the Music." *The New York Times*, June 6, 1990.

WENDY LEE GRAMM

"Commodity Futures Trading Commission Annual Report 1989." Washington, D.C.: Commodity Futures Trading Commission.

Craig, Jim. "Wendy Gramm—An image breaker." *Texas Weekly Magazine*, October 13, 1985.

Green, Larry and Risen, James. "U.S. Indicts 46 Traders in Commodities Probe." *Los Angeles Times*, August 3, 1989.

Jennings, Diane. "Wendy Gramm." *Dallas Morning News*, February 10, 1985.

"Nomination of Wendy L. Gramm. Hearing before the Committee on Agriculture, Nutrition, and Forestry, United

States Senate." Washington, D.C.: U.S. Government
Printing Office, 1988.

DANIEL K. INOUYE

Alexander, Hayley. "Man of Action, Defender of Peace." *Rice*,
June, 1988.
Inouye, Daniel K. with Elliot, Lawrence. *Journey to Washington*.
Englewood Cliffs, New Jersey: Prentice Hall, 1967.
Lipman, Victor. "Dan Inouye." *Honolulu Magazine*, July,
1985.

MAXINE HONG KINGSTON

Hoang, Hanh. "Great American Novelist." *Transpacific*, May/
June, 1990.
Iwata, Edward. "Word Warriors." *Los Angeles Times*, June 24,
1990.

JUNE KURAMOTO

Kitano, Harry H. L. and Daniels, Roger. *Asian Americans:
Emerging Minorities*. Englewood Cliffs, New Jersey: Pren-
tice Hall, 1988.
Niiya, Brian T. "Hiroshima: Sansei & the Search for Japanese
American Music." *Tozai Times*, April, 1989.
Sing, Bill and Seriguchi, Karen. *Asian Pacific Americans*. Los
Angeles: National Conference of Christians and Jews,
Asian American Journalists Association, and Association
of Asian Pacific American Artists, 1989.

HAING NGOR

Lu, Elizabeth. "For Haing Ngor, Sorrow Marks a Return
Home." *Los Angeles Times*, September 12, 1989.
McMillan, Penelope. "By Day, His Job May Be Routine—

But by Night, He's a Celebrity." *Los Angeles Times*, May 8, 1985.

Ngor, Haing with Warner, Roger. *A Cambodian Odyssey*. New York: Warner Books, 1987.

Wood, Daniel B. "His Life Is Cambodia's Story." *The Christian Science Monitor*, March 31, 1988.

DUSTIN NGUYEN

Nakashima, John. "Dustin Nguyen: His Reel Adventures Pale in Comparison to His Real Life Story." *Asiam*, August, 1987.

"Racin' Dustin." *Transpacific*, May/June, 1990.

Silden, Isobel. "Dustin Nguyen: TV Cop." *Asiam*, May/June, 1989.

Vespa, Mary with Alexander, Michael. "A Survivor of the Fall of Saigon, '21 Jump Street's' Dustin Nguyen Relives his Ordeal on TV." *People*, April 25, 1988.

ELLISON S. ONIZUKA

Ogawa, Dennis M. and Grant, Glenn. *Ellison S. Onizuka: A Remembrance*. Kailua-Kona, Hawaii: Onizuka Memorial Committee, Signature Publishing, and Mutual Publishing, 1986.

I. M. PEI

Filler, Martin. "Power Pei." *Vanity Fair*, September, 1989.

Goldberger, Paul. "Winning Ways of I. M. Pei." *The New York Times*, May 20, 1979.

"Hall of Fame" in "Talk of the Town" column. *The New Yorker*, February 22, 1988.

Morita, Tad. "Ozymandias." *Transpacific*, September/October, 1989.

Walter, Betsy. "I. M. Pei: Architect of Elegant Rationalism." *Belle*, September/October, 1980.

SAMUEL C. C. TING

Mann, Charles C. "Armies of Physicists Struggle to Discover Proof of a Scot's Brainchild." *Smithsonian*, March, 1989.

"The Nobel Prizes" in "Science and the Citizen" column. *Scientific American*, December, 1976.

Ting, Samuel C. C. "On Becoming a Physicist." Article supplied by Dr. Ting's office, Massachusetts Institute of Technology, Cambridge, Massachusetts.

AN WANG

Berney, Karen. "An Wang: Getting to the Essentials." *Nation's Business*, December, 1987.

Cho, Yong Bum. "Wang & Son: Inside the Wang Empire." *Asiam*, May/June, 1989.

Perry, Nancy J. "Lasting Fame, Honorable Invention." *Fortune*, April 25, 1988.

Wang, An with Linden, Eugene. *Lessons*. Reading, Massachusetts: Addison-Wesley, 1986.

Index